Counseling Those with Eating Disorders

RESOURCES FOR
CHRISTIAN COUNSELING

RESOURCES FOR CHRISTIAN COUNSELING

(*Other volumes forthcoming*)

VOLUME FOUR

Counseling Those with Eating Disorders

RAYMOND E. VATH, M.D.

RESOURCES FOR
CHRISTIAN COUNSELING

—————— General Editor ——————

Gary R. Collins, Ph.D.

WORD PUBLISHING
Dallas · London · Sydney · Singapore

Unless otherwise noted, Scripture quotations are from The Amplified Bible, Old Testament, copyright © 1962, 1964 by Zondervan Publishing House, and are used with permission. Scriptures identified as TLB are from The Living Bible, copyright 1971 by Tyndale House Publishers; those identified as NKJV are from the New King James Version, copyright 1979, 1980, 1982 by Thomas Nelson, Inc., Publishers; those identified as KJV are from the King James Version. Used with permission.

Weight tables are from the Metropolitan Life Insurance Company, copyright 1983, and are used with permission.

DSM III diagnostic criteria are from the American Psychiatric Association, Diagnostic and Statistical Manual of Mental Disorders, Third Edition, Washington, D.C., APA, 1980, and are used with permission.

Library of Congress Cataloging-in-Publication Data

Vath, Raymond E.
  Counseling those with eating disorders.

  (Resources for Christian counseling; v. 4)
  Bibliography: p.
  Includes index.
  1. Pastoral counseling.   2. Eating disorders—
Psychological aspects.   3. Eating disorders—Religious
aspects—Christianity.   I. Title.   II. Series.
BV4012.2.V37   1986   616.85′2   86–22427
ISBN 0–8499–0583–4

      9 8 FG 9 8 7 6 5 4 3 2

Printed in the United States of America

This commandment I give you,
that you love one another.

Jesus Christ

The secret of caring for patients
is caring for patients.

Paracelsus

CONTENTS

EDITOR'S PREFACE

I NEVER REALLY APPRECIATED the seriousness and reality of eating disorders until I stood recently next to a grieving father and gazed at the body of his twenty-year-old daughter. The dimmed lights and flower-decked quiet of the funeral home were in stark contrast to the boundless energy and vivacious spirit that this young lady had shown only a few months previously. She had read about Pat Boone's daughter who overcame anorexia, but sometimes she felt more like singer Karen Carpenter whose death had shocked fans all over the world. Counseling had helped my friend's daughter, but bodies cannot go on forever when they lack proper nutrients. One night her heart simply stopped. Neither immediate CPR nor the frantic efforts of paramedics could get it going again.

During her short life, this girl and her family had been active in our church. Members of the congregation rallied around those who were grieving, but many of us wondered if we had failed to give the earlier help that might have prevented a tragedy. Could pastors, youth leaders, lay people, and other Christian counselors have an influence in helping those who struggle with eating disorders?

Twenty years ago, few people had heard of anorexia or bulimia. Pastoral counselors rarely encountered people with eating disorders, and deaths like that of the young lady from our church were almost unknown.

But that has all changed. Eating disorders have become a major health problem, especially among young women. Most large churches, and many that are smaller, have families who struggle over the erratic eating habits of a family member. Nothing could be less effective and more insensitive than telling these families to ignore the problem, or confronting young people with their "sinful eating habits" and telling them to start eating properly. As this book so clearly shows, eating disorders are a disease that must be treated with care and competence.

When the people at Word Books approached me about editing a series of books on counseling, anorexia and bulimia were among the first topics to be mentioned. "This is becoming a major problem in the church and society," somebody suggested, and everyone agreed that a book on eating disorders should be one of the first to appear in this series.

Where does one find a qualified Christian writer for such a book? I knew people who had counseled those with eating disorders, but it seemed important to find an author who had developed expertise in this area. When a colleague suggested the name of Raymond Vath, I remembered that he was the psychiatrist described in Cherry Boone O'Neill's best-selling book *Starving for Attention.* When I met Ray and Joanne Vath in Seattle, I found two warm, gracious, deeply committed Christians who are actively involved in their local church. Dr. Vath is acknowledged as a leading figure in the treatment of eating disorders, and I was delighted when he agreed to write a book for the Resources for Christian Counseling series.

As every counselor is well aware, we currently are living in the midst of a "counseling boom." Surely there has never been a time in history when so many people are aware of psychological issues, concerned about personal problems, interested in psychological writings, and willing to talk about their insecurities, inadequacies, and intimate concerns. Within only a few decades we have seen the birth of a great host of theories, degree programs, books, seminars, articles, new journals, radio programs, films, and tape presentations that deal with counseling-related issues. Numerous counselors have appeared, some with good training and great competence, but others with little sensitivity and not much awareness of what they are trying to accomplish.

Perhaps it is not surprising that the counseling field is confusing to many people, threatening to some, and often criticized both within the church and without. Nevertheless, people still struggle with psychological and spiritual problems, stress is both a personal and social issue, and many seek help from counselors.

And how does the counselor keep abreast of latest developments? Many turn to books, but it is difficult to know which of the many volumes on the market are of good quality and which are not. The Resources for Christian Counseling series is an attempt to provide books that give clearly written, practical, up-to-date overviews of the issues faced by contemporary Christian counselors. Written by counseling experts, each of whom has a strong Christian commitment, the books are intended to be examples of accurate psychology and careful use of Scripture. Each is intended to have a clear evangelical perspective, careful documentation, a strong practical orientation, and freedom from the sweeping statements and undocumented rhetoric that sometimes characterize books in the counseling field. All of the Resources for Christian Counseling books will have similar bindings and together they will comprise a complete encyclopedia of Christian counseling.

Portions of Raymond Vath's book may be difficult to read because of the medical terms. The author simplifies complicated issues, however, and argues that when counselors—including pastoral counselors—know little about the physical aspects of anorexia and bulimia they also make little progress in working with counselees and families who are often very knowledgeable.

I can think of no person more qualified to write this book

than Raymond Vath. Known internationally as an expert in the understanding and treatment of eating disorders, he is much in demand both as a counselor and a speaker. His book combines the knowledge and insights of a competent professional with the sensitivity and compassion of a committed follower of Jesus Christ.

All of us will benefit from this important book. It is my prayer that the following pages will help churches and families avoid the loss that our congregation felt when one of our young members died because of an eating disorder.

Gary R. Collins, Ph.D.
Kildeer, Illinois

INTRODUCTION

WHEN I WAS first asked to write a book on eating disorders, I struggled with two choices: Should I write a how-to-treat book or a book that explains the attitudes and the principles that have been effective in treating over two hundred eating disorder cases. I've noticed that "how to" books are often used as a "cloak of righteousness" by counselors who attempt to adopt the behaviors of another counselor without looking at the underlying attitudes and concepts from which those behaviors should come. This frequently leads to subtle, or not so subtle, inconsistencies in the relationship between the counselor and the client. Because these inconsistencies can impair recovery, I have chosen the latter approach.

This choice is based not only on my own experience with clients but it also includes the input of a number of other therapists and counselors including several whom I supervise. We have concluded that if appropriate attitudes and concepts can be identified as valuable and true, and then incorporated into the very personality of the counselor, the counselor will indeed become an instrument of healing for people who are experiencing eating disorders. This is especially apparent in the treatment of people with anorexia who are often rather brittle. Unless handled properly, the outcome will be further deterioration and even death. On the other hand, there is no greater reward than knowing that your life has brought healing and life to another human being.

Because of my approach, the reader may sometimes feel frustrated about a seeming lack of direction in the treatment of eating disorders. But I am convinced that when your own sense of direction is unclear, it is time for an attitude check and for a recommitment to a collaborative model that includes the client, the family and/or other consultants.

In writing this book I found it difficult to present the complicated interplay of dynamics found in these disorders. Although I have tried to separate the various issues as I analyzed them, no clear boundaries exist in real life. As will become apparent, some issues contain other issues that overlap and recur again and again. This may at times seem redundant, but therapy often involves repetition as the grip of old habits is broken. If you keep in mind that this only points to the complicated intertwining of the causes of human behavior and if you can remember to think multidimensionally, this becomes easier to handle.

As I read the finished manuscript, I noticed that I have recreated the feeling that I experience in therapy with clients. There is a sense of two steps forward and one step back, recurrent clarification of issues, and reinforcement of positive change. If the reader can approximate this in his or her work with clients, the results will be satisfactory.

This book is a result of a collaborative effort and I am indebted so much to many people for the information that is presented. Of course, the greatest debt is due to those early patients who patiently waited for me to gain the knowledge and experience to help them, and who were the greatest source of insight into the nature of these disorders. I am also indebted to the many authors found in the bibliography who have shared their information with us all. Through their sharing, a clearer picture of eating disorders is emerging that will enable the therapeutic community to treat these problems with greater efficiency and effectiveness.

I also owe much to my colleagues, Doctors Janet Berg, Richard Hedges, Wally Hodges, Kim Lampson Reiff, Robert Wills, Sig Weedman, and our nutritionist Dan Reiff. The reader owes a debt of gratitude to my son-in-law, David Montgomery; my sister, Helen Konyha, Dan O'Neill, and Evelyn Bence for editing the manuscript and making it more readable. I would like to express special appreciation to my office manager, Glenda Ewell, for the many hours at the word processor. Without her dedicated and efficient work, I would not have dared to add the burden of a book to my very busy practice. I also owe much to the General Editor for this series, Gary Collins, whose wisdom and experience guided me along the way.

Patient stories are often a composite of several patient situations and patient identities are protected by the use of pseudonyms.

PART ONE

THE NATURE, CAUSES, AND CONSEQUENCES OF ANOREXIA NERVOSA AND BULIMIA

CHAPTER ONE

THE STORY OF EATING DISORDERS

BECKY WAS TWENTY-ONE when she first came to consult with me. She revealed that she had battled an eating disorder for five years, its onset occurring after a sudden weight gain to 138 pounds which she felt was too much for her five-foot four-inch frame. She stated that her two sisters and her mother continually struggled with weight control. After several partially successful attempts at dieting, coupled with vigorous exercise, she had seemed to have a breakthrough and her weight had fallen below 110 pounds, giving her a powerful sense of mastery and control not previously experienced. At any gain in weight, however, even as little as half a pound, she would experience intense anxiety which could only be relieved by further weight loss caused by more severe exercising and dieting. She would control cravings by limiting herself to a narrow list of nonfattening foods, mainly salads and vegetables.

Initially she had received many compliments from friends and family, especially from boys in her high school. Even the family doctor had congratulated her for the good example that she was setting for the other family members; he had also pointed out to all the benefits of weight reduction and control. Later on, as her weight fell below one hundred pounds, the compliments had diminished, but by then the sense of being in control had become more important than the opinions of others.

In addition, there seemed to be a very real burst of energy and she was able to exercise compulsively with little sign of fatigue. Others had admired her industry and commitment to good health. She had required less sleep than before and was able to get unusual amounts of school work completed. Her grades, while always good, had improved even more. During this period she had graduated from high school with honors, just before her eighteenth birthday, and had received a scholarship to a good college. This furthered her belief that "thin is better" and "to be thin is to be successful."

During her first year of college, Becky's weight dropped below ninety pounds and her life began to deteriorate. First, she noticed that her endurance began to wane. Her menstrual periods stopped, but she didn't miss them, her weight now more important than female physiology. She became irritable, snapping at her parents and friends. Because of her embarrassment over these new behaviors, she began to avoid social contacts.

With these changes, her family began to express worry about her health. They expressed the opinion that she had carried her weight control measures too far, and reminded her about moderation in all things. Her father, a very successful attorney whose busy practice kept him relatively uninvolved with the family except for brief vacations, offered to buy her an expensive sports car if she would just give up her funny diets. After that she felt he really didn't know her and did not understand her struggles. Her mother, with whom she felt closer, tried to help by preparing what used to be Becky's favorite meals. When they were only partially eaten, the mother would ask what was wrong.

Becky attempted to regain the good feelings initially associated with her weight control. Once again, exercise became frantic; her interest in food, recipes, and meal planning became an obsession. As she looked for the solution to her growing sense of failure, she stopped eating with the family, claiming too much school work which "she would do while she ate." It would also reduce the opportunity for family members to comment on her increasingly unusual eating habits, and she would not have to endure attempts on their part to encourage her to eat more than she wanted. Because school was the one area in which she had attained some success, the family was reluctant to interfere with this decision.

The family, who regularly attended church, asked the pastor for help. Although by this time Becky was attending church irregularly (as part of her social withdrawal), she did see the pastor who quietly and kindly stated that her body was a temple of God. With honest concern about her health, he encouraged her to take better care of it. She did attempt for a period of time to eat a more balanced diet and did stop her weight loss for almost three months. Then when the weight loss continued she was too embarrassed to go back and see him again.

When her weight fell below eighty pounds, she noticed an intolerance to cold, even when others were comfortable. To compensate, she began to wear warm, fleecy sweat suits which not only kept her warmer but also hid her now emaciated shape, so comments from others diminished. She then began to experience a dizziness and lightheadedness when getting up from a chair, and feelings of weakness occurred with greater frequency.

Whereas she previously had resisted seeing the family doctor, she now went willingly. He was appalled at her deterioration and, suspecting a hidden malignancy such as leukemia, began a thorough medical evaluation. When those tests were negative, further tests were done to find a hidden infection or an endocrine imbalance. These tests revealed only a mild thyroid deficiency.

About this time, her mother noticed an article about eating disorders in a popular magazine. The description of the illness, anorexia nervosa, matched Becky's condition and when she showed it to Becky, she agreed. Finally, the problem at least had a name.

The family doctor inquired about treatments for eating disorders and, after much searching, he found a program at a nearby medical center. At first Becky was reluctant to enter such a program; if she had been able to fool her own doctor for several years, if her so-successful family was powerless to help her, if her church had seemingly given up, as no one called or inquired about her well-being, then her problem must be untreatable. Because of her own anxiety about her obvious physical deterioration, she agreed to enter the hospital program, but with great reservation.

Upon admission, she met a businesslike, organized staff whose efficiency and systematic approach helped her feel more secure. Her physical examination was thorough but without unnecessary tests that her own doctor had performed. It confirmed her weight at seventy-eight pounds, her blood pressure at 88/30, marked muscle wasting, and a fine growth of facial hair. Throughout the exam she shivered with cold, although the room was a moderate temperature, and as soon as possible she returned to the warmth of her fleecy sweat suit. Except for a slight anemia, a low serum protein of 5.2, and a low blood sugar of 68, the remaining laboratory tests were normal. Her electrocardiogram showed small amplitude of the QRS complexes indicating a small heart, and this was confirmed by the chest x-ray.

She felt relieved to have someone specifically identify that her body was not functioning normally, and that someone could explain some of her symptoms.

She met with a nutritionist and attempted to reconstruct her recent diet. Because of growing trust, she decided to be as honest as she could, and as a result of this evaluation it was estimated that her unbalanced diet consisted of four hundred to five hundred calories per day. It was estimated that at her current weight, a maintenance diet would require nine hundred calories per day. A weight gain of a pound a week would require four hundred calories a day more. She was, therefore, started on thirteen hundred calories a day.

They explained that because of her weakened condition, Becky would have to have bed rest until her weight increased. This would also reduce the calorie consumption of exercise. Social contact, including telephone access, would also be restricted until she gained fifteen pounds. When she gained five pounds she would be allowed to attend a group meeting for patients with eating disorders. The bed rest until her health improved made sense, for that's the way most hospital patients are treated. The restriction of social contact did not. Because the staff seemed to know what they were doing, however, she decided to cooperate.

As she attempted to eat the thirteen hundred calories per day, the first real problem arose. This diet nearly tripled her food intake and immediately after eating she became bloated and nauseated. Soon she vomited up her meal. The nurse, whom she called for help, claimed that Becky was not cooperating with the program and decreed that she would have to eat her meals in the presence of staff who would then remain with her for an hour after each meal. The nutritionist was called and made the concession of providing more frequent and smaller meals consisting of foods easier to digest. Although the nausea was still present, at least she could avoid vomiting.

During the night of the fifth day, Becky awakened with a panicky feeling that she couldn't get her breath. She was afraid to call for help for fear that she would again be accused of being uncooperative or manipulative; so she sat up struggling for breath for nearly two hours before calling for help. When the night nurse came, the visible distress mobilized action. The internist on call came and immediately diagnosed the signs of congestive heart failure. There was fluid in her lungs. Her ankles were swollen, and when a finger was pressed against them, a small little pit remained.

The doctor said he had recently read an article by a Dr. Powers about heart failure caused by too rapid a refeeding of persons with anorexia. He explained to Becky that when a person starves, he or she starves all over. Not only do the visible skeletal muscles get small, but the heart muscle also weakens. Other studies have shown that if the refeeding diet is too high in carbohydrates, the problem is aggravated. Becky's diet was immediately reduced to eight hundred calories a day to be increased by one hundred calories as tolerated. No further cardiovascular problems occurred. The experience did shake Becky's confidence in the program, however, and she decided to be more cautious about sharing control of her illness in the future. When she reached eighty-three pounds, she was allowed to leave her room to attend the group meetings. She faced this with mixed feelings. She was apprehensive at the thought of talking openly about her behaviors and feelings, but curiously looking forward to ending the social isolation.

At the meeting, Becky was pleased to find six other women who were also experiencing struggles with food. She felt for the first time as though others understood her struggle even though they also seemed unsure about what course of action to take.

Days passed and Becky's weight slowly but steadily increased. The doctor in charge of her case set a target goal: when Becky reached one hundred fifteen pounds she would be considered for discharge. That seemed extremely high, almost unattainable, but she decided to do the best she could. As her weight neared one hundred pounds, she was allowed to exercise again. At first, she felt that she had become even more weakened by the four weeks of bed rest, but with the increased weight and exercise, her strength rapidly returned. Her blood pressure crept up to 105/60 and the dizziness left.

She found herself spending more and more time with the other women from the group. Their after-hours discussions were even more informative than the scheduled meetings in the presence of staff. When unsupervised, the women felt that they could be more open with each other, since those who had book knowledge and no personal experience of eating disorders seemed not able to understand.

In one of these after-hour discussions Becky first learned of vomiting as a means of weight control. At first it seemed foreign to think of a behavior that had always been a sign of sickness as a potential ally in the battle against weight. She learned that four women in the group were diagnosed as having bulimia, experiencing the binge and purge behaviors.

During the weeks that followed, her weight continued to increase until it plateaued at about one hundred eight pounds and would seem to increase no further. This brought further pressure from the staff who stated that unless weight gain continued, some of her privileges would again be removed.

Instead, Becky complained to her parents that although her

weight had indeed increased and her health was much better, she was really getting little help with her problems of coping with life; she questioned whether continued work with the program was worth the rather high cost. She had accurately perceived that her parents were having similar feelings and soon they too were demanding that she be released from the hospital. Her doctor told the family that in his opinion discharge was premature for they had not attained the goal of one hundred fifteen pounds. He feared that the recovery that had been made was still quite tenuous and the risk of relapse was quite high. On the other hand, he stated he could not hold her against her will and when Becky insisted she be released, she was.

In order to prove the doctor and the staff wrong, Becky worked doubly hard to avoid weight loss by eating more normally and by exercising appropriately. Yet one day during the second month following her discharge from the hospital, in a fit of boredom, she found herself returning to the refrigerator again and again, especially attracted to a half-gallon of ice cream. As the evening progressed, she felt driven to consume the entire half-gallon and then turn to a package of cookies which vanished at an alarming rate.

When these sweets were gone, she felt bloated, slightly nauseated, and certainly disgusted with herself, but she tried to go to bed to sleep it off. But the discomfort of her dilated stomach would not let her sleep. After an hour and a half of tossing and turning, she found her thoughts going back to the group discussions on relieving oneself by forced vomiting. She saw this as her way out and, although her first attempts at vomiting were awkward and totally repulsive, after she was done retching, she did experience a strange calm and an enormous relief from the uncomfortable, bloated feeling.

Becky resolved to maintain better control and to try harder to eat and live normally, and was successful for almost two weeks. But then, after a growing period of tension and nervousness, she started calming herself with food, especially sweets. Once again she ate more than she had anticipated and at a much more rapid pace, and once again she felt bloated. She sought relief through vomiting which worked better this time than before.

As the months passed, she settled into this cycle of binging and purging interspersed with periods of attempts at control and found herself strangely anticipating the pleasures of feeling totally satiated and yet knowing that relief could be found so quickly. Unfortunately, the episodes began to happen more and more frequently and brought on new experiences that were highly disturbing. One evening after a particularly difficult binge and purge episode, she experienced a very strong feeling of fear. She felt short of breath and her heart seemed to race. She also experienced an overwhelming feeling of weakness.

This experience unsettled her and she felt it would be well to consult the family doctor once more. When he met her, she stated that she was able to maintain her weight fairly constantly between one hundred five and one hundred ten pounds and that she was glad the anorexia was over. She described her symptoms to him and he inquired if there were any unusual stresses in her life that were causing problems. She did say that she was having trouble in one of her college courses. When the physical examination and laboratory studies showed no problems other than a slightly low potassium level, the doctor assumed that her symptoms were related to her stress and encouraged her to take a lighter load the following quarter.

In her heart Becky knew that there was more the doctor should have known, but she was too embarrassed to tell him. Because she suspected that his advice would not be very helpful, she did not follow it, except for his recommendation that she increase her consumption of fruit and fruit juices to raise her potassium level. To her surprise she found this did reduce her symptoms and her craving for sweets. For a time, with careful control, the binging did diminish to about once a week.

Then, with final exams approaching and with the promise of a new job, her control started to slip. With dread, she found the bulimia increasing once more.

About this time, an event occurred that prompted a change for Becky. While sitting in class one day, she looked up and her eyes met the casual glance of Greg, a handsome and friendly classmate. She was a bit flustered that their silent exchange seemed more than a casual glance. Still, there was something comforting in the warm friendliness she read in his eyes.

At the end of the class, they exchanged pleasantries. By the end of the week they had their first date. Now faced with "love at first sight," Becky felt marvelous but increasingly fearful. What if he found out about her secret compulsion? It was that fear and the decision to master this problem once and for all that led her to my office, asking for my help.

With such a story that rather classically describes the struggles of a victim of an eating disorder, where does one begin to look for causes and solutions? What, if anything, helps? It is to answer such questions that this book has been written.

CHAPTER TWO

EATING IS A COMPLEX ACTIVITY

JESUS SAID that it is easier for a camel to go through the eye of a needle than it is for a rich man to enter into the kingdom of heaven. Truly, affluence breeds many problems and one in particular has been especially neglected by the church: eating disorders. Anorexia nervosa and bulimia are not found in populations where famine is common, but frequently emerge in societies blessed with abundance.

THERE'S SO MUCH WE DON'T KNOW

Although the Mosaic laws always advocated good health and the church more recently has made strong statements against smoking and excesses of drinking, it is amazing how we fall silent in the area of dietary excesses. We have not learned from the example of a wise Daniel who set up a scientific experiment that convinced the king's men to allow Daniel to eat a simple but healthy diet (Dan. 1:8–19). We have allowed these excesses to go unchallenged in the church often because of ignorance, our own lack of discipline, and an inadequate commitment to helping others exercise better stewardship of their health. What makes this all the more difficult is the fact that food, an essential need of mankind, is an area of human experience where inadequate or inappropriate training has traditionally abounded. Major exceptions to these statements are found only in some of the smaller denominations such as the Adventists, who have made nutrition a significant part of their theology.

The medical community is beginning to address these issues: Since 1970 the American death rate due to heart disease has declined 21 percent, and due to stroke, 32 percent.[1] These changes are said to be due to the recent emphasis on simpler diets and aerobic exercise, coupled with a greater adherence to warnings about smoking and excessive drinking.[2]

In 1970, after I had been in practice for about a year, a very thin, distressed woman came to my office seeking help. Although I had had some exposure to anorexia nervosa during my psychiatric training, I was quite aware that I knew very little about the disease process. A review of the literature led me to several simplistic theories, but none of these seemed sufficient to explain the complexity of the illness that bound this troubled woman. Therefore, I embarked on a treatment strategy that Hilde Bruch has recently called the "constructive use of ignorance."[3] This approach, which is theoretically eclectic, suggested that if I read enough and listened long enough the patient would teach me about the illness and together we would find answers to her problem. Perhaps Solomon was correct when he said, "Even the wisest man who says he knows everything, doesn't" (Eccles. 8:17 TLB).

ALCOHOLISM AND EATING DISORDERS HAVE SIMILARITIES

My own training included a rather intense period of research in the area of alcoholism under the sponsorship of Dr. Joan K. Jackson, an internationally recognized expert in the field.

This experience taught me that alcoholism is a complex illness with many aspects including sociocultural, genetic, intrapsychic, interpersonal, and physical, all of which need to be addressed if the alcoholic is to be helped. One of the first bits of information that stood out to me was the similarity between the two disease processes.

- There is a compulsive aspect to both diseases.
- They are self-destructive in that they endanger life.
- They involve guilt and fear that lead to much denial and covering of the nature of the illnesses.
- Both can be viewed as slow forms of suicide.
- The families are usually involved in a critical, punitive manner in an attempt to rescue the victims from their illnesses.
- There are usually family histories of mood disorders.
- Both diseases are also strongly influenced by societal values and expectations.

My own observations, confirmed by others, indicate there is a fairly high overlap of the two illnesses in that many people with bulimia also have alcohol and drug problems.[4]

In the area of alcoholism, I've been taught the treatment approach should be multidimensional with a strategy aimed at overcoming the many complicated factors involved. This process results in the best outcome. I began to apply this approach to my first anorexic patient, and, to my amazement, she began to recover. Because of my inexperience, her recovery was not complete, yet she was able to make a reasonably satisfactory adjustment to life, and at a more stable weight. Because of our success together, a few other such patients appeared in my office and we similarly approached the problems.

As I continued to carefully listen to the patients and also review the literature, I developed a list of crucial issues that appeared to be present to varying degrees in all of my patients with eating disorders, both anorexia nervosa and bulimia.

PIECES OF THE PUZZLE

Perfectionism These individuals have unreasonable standards or expectations of themselves and go to unusual lengths in their attempts to attain those standards.

Low Self-Esteem Because the standards are so excessive, they develop severe self-esteem problems when they fall short of their expectations and, therefore, feel worthless and unlovable.

Sexual Identity Confusion As a component of low self-esteem, they often experience significant sexual identity confusion in not being sure of what kind of man or woman they would like to be as they develop into maturity.

Depression Because of the disparity between their expectations and their perceived self, they are predisposed to anxious depressions. This is usually reinforced by a family history of depression. In the majority of the cases, a first order relative (mother, father, brother, or sister) has experienced illness associated with depression.

Deception Because of their high and unmet expectations, they often are burdened with guilt, and make serious attempts to hide their symptoms, often by engaging in the abnormal eating behaviors in private, and sometimes by stealing food or laxatives.

Power Struggle When the illness is discovered by the family, often a significant battle begins as the family attempts to force the victim of the illness to give up the symptoms of the disease using threats, criticism, and punishment.

Interdependency Wanting to be the perfect parents, the mother and father often attempt to control the patient into being the perfect child. Because they may look to the child for validation and gratification in some areas of their own uncertainty, it becomes difficult for parents to allow the child to undergo the normal process of separation. On the other hand, the dominated anorexic and bulimic child has little self-confidence and, therefore, views the family in a very ambivalent way, wanting to leave and yet afraid to actually disengage.

Physiologic Problems There is much data about additional biochemical and physiologic problems in eating disorders, and medical scientists are still sorting through the data, attempting to determine which are causes and which are effects.

Each of the above factors in eating disorders will be the

subject of a separate chapter, presenting concepts by which each factor can be evaluated and therapeutically addressed.

THE KARPMAN TRIANGLE

A very useful concept in understanding the complexity of the dynamics of the factors listed is the Karpman Triangle.[5] This is an interactional process in which people rotate among three positions: persecutor, victim, and rescuer. This triangle is commonly found in families of alcoholics, and Claude Steiner has described the process vividly in *Games Alcoholics Play.*[6] In the persecutory phase, the parents often resort to intimidation and threats to arouse guilt in their attempt to get the patient to stop the abnormal eating practices. Sadly, these are the very approaches that have led to the perfectionism and low self-esteem in the first place. When this backfires and the patient becomes acutely ill, the family moves into the role of rescuer, giving the patient the "power" to persecute the then victimized family. The patient may also be using the illness to rescue the family from other unresolved conflicts, by drawing conflict to herself.

As we discuss the Karpman Triangle and issues relating to medical problems of eating disorders, you may encounter information and concepts beyond your education or experience. Rather than skipping over such sections, try seeking out someone who is medically trained and ask for any necessary explanations. Not only will this insight add credibility to your counsel, but it will help establish a healthy, collaborative relationship between the ministerial and medical communities. It is my observation that when people of good will begin to work together, even difficult goals can generally be attained.

One important concept that must be understood for anyone working with patients with eating disorders is that the illness's complexity makes it necessary that patients be treated in the context of a multidisciplinary team involving therapists, physicians, dieticians, and family and spiritual counselors. I will soon point out to you that there are several special areas in the treatment of eating disorders where a knowledgeable pastoral counselor can be especially effective if a complete cure is to be obtained. It is increasingly apparent to me that Solomon was correct when he wrote, "In the multitude of counselors there is safety" (Prov. 11:14).

During my sixteen years of practice treating patients with eating disorders, I've watched the growth of interest in the field and the resulting rapidly expanding data base. This is resulting in a greater understanding of these illnesses so we can treat them with greater efficiency and effectiveness.

CHAPTER THREE

DIAGNOSTIC CRITERIA

ANY DISCUSSION OF AN ILLNESS must attempt to address the criteria by which the illness can be recognized. Unfortunately, there is still some lack of precision in the diagnosis of eating disorders. For the sake of simplicity, I'm presenting two approaches, the first being the consensus of the psychiatric community as stated in the *Diagnostic and Statistical Manual of Mental Disorders–III*. The eating disorders section was written by Craig Johnson of Northwestern University and is the standard of diagnosis used in most scientific studies. The second approach, a descriptive diagnosis, is a consensus of both lay organizations and the scientific community in an attempt to add further description of signs and symptoms to make the recognition of the illnesses easier.

DSM–III

In the *Diagnostic and Statistical Manual of Mental Disorders–III*, anorexia nervosa is described as an illness characterized by "intense fear of becoming obese, which does not diminish as weight loss progresses; disturbance of body image, e.g. claiming to 'feel fat' even when emaciated; weight loss of at least 25 percent of original body weight or, if under 18 years of age, weight loss from original body weight plus projected weight gain expected from growth charts may be combined to make the 25 percent; refusal to maintain body weight over a minimal normal weight for age and height; and no known physical illness that would account for the weight loss." [1]

DSM–III defines bulimia as "recurrent episodes of binge eating (rapid consumption of a large amount of food in a discrete period of time, usually less than three hours), and at least three of the following: 1. consumption of high-caloric, easily ingested food during a binge, 2. inconspicuous eating during a binge, 3. termination of such eating by abdominal pain, sleep, social interruption (arrival of people), or self-induced vomiting, 4. repeated attempts to lose weight by severely restrictive diets, self-induced vomiting, or use of cathartics (laxatives) and/or diuretics, 5. frequent weight fluctuations greater than ten pounds due to alternating binges and fasts." There is also "awareness that the eating pattern is abnormal and fear of not being able to stop eating voluntarily." Present also are "depressed mood and self-depreciating thoughts following eating binges. The bulimic episodes are not due to anorexia nervosa or any known physical disorder." [2]

Although obesity is also an eating disorder with many features in common with anorexia nervosa and bulimia, it is a subject that merits a book by itself. It will be addressed only in passing as some of the common features are addressed. Curiously, obesity is not considered a psychiatric illness and does not appear in DSM–III.

DESCRIPTIVE DIAGNOSIS

Anorexia nervosa is an illness characterized by preoccupation with body weight, behaviors directed toward losing weight, and intense fear of gaining weight, coupled with unusual preoccupation with food including bizarre behaviors in handling it. There is often refusal to eat, except for small portions, and a denial of hunger. This leads to significant weight loss consistent with the DSM–III definitions. There may be an exaggerated interest in food and food planning.

Often there is a high energy level coupled with excessive, compulsive exercise with diminished signs of fatigue. Menstrual periods will stop, sometimes as weight loss begins. As weight loss becomes severe, there is an intolerance to cold, especially notable are cold hands and feet. Loss of head hair coupled with a growth of fine body and facial hair may also occur. Pulse rate slows and blood pressure will fall. Constipation is especially common if laxative abuse occurs.

Sooner or later depression will occur, frequently coupled with thoughts of suicide. Social withdrawal usually occurs early as the victim becomes alienated from family and friends alike.

Bulimia is an illness with recurrent, compulsive episodes of binge eating followed by self-induced vomiting and/or purging with laxatives and/or diuretics. Its symptoms include secretive binge eating, menstrual irregularities, swollen paratid (mumps) glands, cardiac irregularities, fluctuations of weight due to alternating binges and fasts, and a fear of the inability to stop eating voluntarily. Guilt and depression are almost invariably present after a binge, and despair to the point of suicide is not uncommon. Many persons are able to maintain work and an apparently normal social life, keeping their secret habit well hidden for years.

Both anorexia nervosa and bulimia are serious, life-threatening disorders with risk to health and to life itself. These illnesses usually begin during adolescence or young adulthood, sometimes as an aftermath of dieting. They may also begin after a loss, or a disappointment in romance. Mainly, white females from middle- and upper middle-class families are affected. The parents are usually conscientious, educated, well-meaning people who are high achievers themselves. One or both parents are often health conscious and concerned with diet. Not uncommonly one or both parents tend toward perfectionism, being quite intolerant of error and failure in others as well as themselves.

It is my impression that patients with anorexia tend to be

inflexible, and overcontrolled, able to resist powerful hunger. Some feel that a basic underlying personality of the anorexic client is obsessive-compulsive neurosis.[3] Patients with bulimia tend to be impulsive and undercontrolled, unable to resist appetite, even when modest. There is also, however, a group of patients that seem to vacillate between the two disorders, dieting rigorously at times, binging uncontrollably at other times.

Anorexia nervosa and bulimia are ten to twenty times more common among women than among men. Because of the preponderance of women in the incidence of eating disorders, feminine pronouns have been used when referring to persons with the problem.

Although I have treated male patients with eating disorders who were heterosexual, there is an impression that the association of homosexuality and eating disorders among males is higher than one would normally expect. This is not surprising if, as I have stated, confusion about sexual identity is a factor in the development of an eating disorder. Because the causes of homosexuality are uncertain, and its treatment yet controversial, its presence may complicate the treatment of the eating disorder because of the difficulty in finding an environment with unconditional love and attitudes devoid of punishment.

CHAPTER FOUR

WHAT EATING DISORDERS DO TO THE BODY

Eating disorders affect the body in a large variety of ways. Because many of the effects are different for anorexia as compared with bulimia, it is best to discuss them separately, even though some patients have a combination of both illnesses.

Anorexia Nervosa

Mental Function

Without adequate nutrition, the brain cannot function normally. When people have the delusional idea that they are fat, when they are not, perhaps this is at least partially caused by a processing error of a starving brain. Indeed, for the starved victim of anorexia, a return to normal weight often reduces or eliminates the delusion.

That judgment can be affected by the lack of vitamins has long been known. Vitamin B_6 deficiency is known to cause pellagra psychosis and Vitamin B_1 deficiency causes Korsakoff's psychosis. Do similar deficiencies exist in anorexia as well?

Compulsive cravings are common in all eating disorders, and we wonder if these might be due to a physiologic hunger for specific missing nutrients including vitamins, minerals, proteins, sugars, and fats. Recent studies have shown that obsessive-compulsive behaviors are responsive to a specific antidepressant medication, chlorimipramine, and this discovery may suggest that specific chemical deficiencies in the brain may contribute to obsessional thinking. The now known association of eating disorders and depression may similarly be related, but other factors are operating as well. This will be clarified further in the chapter on depression.

It is also important to note that in both anorexia and bulimia, patients show a higher incidence of seizure disorders than the general population. Although the cause of this is not known, we are aware that low serum sodium, potassium, and magnesium can cause seizures, as can low blood sugar, and very low blood pressure.

On occasion, an anorexic patient's night vision is impaired, most likely due to a vitamin A deficiency.

Cardiovascular Function

With starvation, the heart shrinks and becomes weak. This will result in low blood pressure and poor organ perfusion, which leads to the impairment of the metabolic process.

The deficiency of sodium, magnesium, calcium, and especially potassium salts prompted by the anorexic's poor diet can cause electrical defects in the heart that can lead to sudden cardiac arrest and death. A very low potassium level is an ominous warning sign.

If the anorexic is using the medicine Ipecac to induce vomiting or to diminish hunger, life-threatening damage to the heart muscle may result. (Ipecac, found in many households, induces vomiting and is an effective treatment in accidental poisioning.)

Digestive Function

With inadequate nutrition, an anorexic patient may have deficiencies in the proteins from which digestive enzymes are made in the pancreas and liver. If these enzymes are not present in adequate quantity, digestion will be impaired. This explains the bloating experienced by most persons with eating disorders. Often such bloating is perceived as weight gain, when it is actually due to indigestion.

The lack of nutrients can also impair the function of the major chemical factory of the body, the liver. If the liver is unable to maintain an adequate level of protein in the bloodstream, the blood's osmotic pressure falls, and water leaks into the peripheral tissues causing edema. Should the fluid accumulate in the abdominal cavity, the pot-bellied appearance, seen in many starving people, results.

For reasons that are not understood, the stomachs of both anorexic and bulimic victims usually empty more slowly than normal, and this contributes to discomfort and to fears of obesity when bloating occurs.

Kidney Function

As a result of a weakened heart, poor perfusion, and poor nutrition, an anorexic patient's kidneys may be unable to clear the blood of toxic wastes, and this failure contributes to further metabolic collapse. This malfunction will also aggravate fluid retention, further overloading a weakened heart. Some persons with anorexia load up on water prior to weighing themselves in session, and this can be one of the precipitating factors in both seizures and cardiac arrest by diluting already diminished concentrations of body salts.

Blood Cell Function

In many cases of anorexia, the production of blood cells is impaired. About half of anorexics have a reduced white blood cell count, about a quarter a low red blood cell count. The former may lead to impaired immunity, the latter to anemia and weakness.

Glandular Function

The thyroid gland is nearly always impaired in anorexia as the body attempts to diminish metabolism and thus conserve tissue. This results in cold intolerance, dry skin, and brittle hair.

When a person's weight drops below about 70 percent of ideal, the body's hormonal function becomes similar to that prior to puberty. Menstrual periods stop and secondary sexual characteristics are lost. Without medical hormonal stimulation, menses may not restart even after weight is regained.

In anorexia, steroid (cortisone) levels are higher than normal. Since this is also found in depression, it is not known whether this is a cause or an effect of the illness. As depression lifts, the steroid level tends to return to normal, and this is sometimes used as an indicator of therapeutic effectiveness of antidepressant medication.

Musculoskeletal Function

In anorexia there is usually a significant loss of calcium from bones and even teeth. There is evidence that this may lead to premature osteoporosis (bone softening) with resulting fracturing and loss of height as vertebrae collapse.

BULIMIA

Mental Function

Compulsive eating is usually stronger in bulimia than in anorexia but may be triggered by the same mechanisms (such as craving for specific nutrients). If purging is excessive, confusion and disorientation may result, usually due to salt and water imbalance. Seizures are also more frequent in bulimia than in anorexia, probably because more salts are lost by vomiting than avoided in starvation.

Cardiovascular Function

Because the salt and water imbalances are often more severe in bulimia, there is probably a greater risk of cardiac arrest than in anorexia. Again, if Ipecac is abused, death may result from its toxic effect on the heart muscle.

Digestive Function

The frequent vomiting in bulimia may result in esophagitis, an inflammation of the esophagus. If the inflamed tissue becomes weakened, it may rupture during a severe vomiting episode. This is a medical emergency and care must be obtained immediately to prevent death. If the esophagitis becomes chronic, the esophagus may become scarred and narrowed. Swallowing will become difficult and surgical treatment necessary.

If laxative abuse becomes excessive, the colon may become weak and dilated which leads to intractable constipation. Restoration to normal function may take years if it occurs at all. The unfortunate reality is that laxatives rarely prevent weight gain unless damage to the small bowel occurs, so that absorption of nutrients is impaired.

A common occurrence in bulimia is the erosion of teeth. The constant bathing of tooth enamel with acidic stomach contents will corrode it away. An early sign of damage is an unexplained tooth pain. Fluoride treatments will slow the damage and diminish the pain, but will not totally prevent it. When the damage becomes severe, loss of teeth may result.

If alcohol abuse is associated with bulimia, liver function may be impaired from both causes, alcohol damage coupled with malnutrition.

Glandular Function

There is a curious effect of bulimia on the paratid (mumps) glands. For reasons that are unknown, these glands swell in bulimia, often giving the patient a chipmunk-like appearance.

Musculoskeletal Function

If excessive vomiting results in low potassium, muscle spasms (tetany) may result, and this may be both painful and frightening to the patient and the family.

Of the two diseases, anorexia nervosa carries the higher risk of death due to the multiple organ traumas that come from starvation. The usual cause of death is heart failure; the weakened heart muscle can no longer keep up with the metabolic demands of the body. Bulimic patients are more apt to die from cardiac arrest (sudden heart stoppage) caused by salt and water imbalance that results from purging. Bulimics also have greater risk from impulse control disorders, including drug and alcohol abuse, which themselves carry a significant morbidity and mortality.

For the physician, it is important to know that in severe cases of both illnesses, not only must serum electrolyte levels be measured, but electrocardiogram (ECG) monitoring is necessary also. A prolonged QT interval is an ominous sign that cardiac arrest may not be far away.[1] It is not necessary for the nonmedical counselor to understand this technically, but many physicians are unaware of the life-saving value of the ECG in eating disorders. If ECGs are not routinely obtained, they should be requested by the patient or her family.

CHAPTER FIVE

APPETITE CONTROL:
ARE ALL CREATED EQUAL?

WITH ALL DUE RESPECT TO THE DECLARATION OF INDEPENDENCE which states that all are created equal, anyone can clearly see that all of us are created quite differently. This is especially true in terms of the effect of eating habits on body structure. Some people don't gain any weight on three thousand calories a day while others can't lose a pound even though they are consuming less than one thousand calories a day.

As a physician, I am intrigued by the wide variety of diets advocated for weight management and good health: high carbohydrate diets, high protein diets, balanced diets, and limited diets (for example, grapefruit). I've come to realize that almost all of these diets help someone, but no one diet has helped everyone. For example, the high carbohydrate diets of Pritikin [1] and Haas [2] may be excellent for athletes but poor for insulin-dependent diabetics.

Many of these differences can be traced back to the incredibly complex variations in genetic material contained in the DNA of the nucleus of every cell in the body. Just as eye color, for example, seems to run in families, with a well-determined genetic inheritance pattern, so it is that body size is largely determined by genetic factors. [3] Unlike eye color, which is permanently fixed, only *potential* body size is genetically determined; environmental factors, such as a deficiency or abundance of food, also play a large part in our physical makeup. In times of famine, even those genetically disposed to obesity will lose weight, but may survive longer than those disposed to slenderness. Such persons living in a culture where a high-vegetable, low-fat diet is consumed, as in the Orient, will have less problems with weight than if they were living in a culture with diets rich in sweets and fats as experienced in rich, French cuisine.

Those who struggle with weight are dealing with very complex factors in the control of appetite. Medical science knows surprisingly little about the control of appetite and the causes of obesity. This lack of knowledge has led all of us, including physicians, to simplistic thinking on the matter of weight. In the past, there was one, simple, black-and-white solution: If you are too fat, eat less! If you are too thin, eat more! This was a grossly inadequate explanation of the struggles faced by many people who worry about their weight. Indeed, it has had a tendency to increase feelings of guilt when people have failed to comply with the demands or to meet the goals based on these simplistic beliefs.

THE HEAD CONTROLS THE MOUTH

We know that there is an appetite control center in the midbrain that, if working correctly, controls a remarkably constant caloric intake. When damaged, it can lead to massive obesity or starvation. When left to its own devices, this appetite center can select an unusually constant amount of calories and, in complex unknown ways, select a reasonably well-balanced diet when a wide choice of foods is available. Many years ago an interesting study discovered that over a period of time, growing children exposed to a wide variety of food of their choice continually selected a well-balanced diet with sufficient calories to maintain good health.[4] Newer studies are clarifying some of the mechanisms by which the brain is able to determine food intake.

A Craving Due to a Mineral Deficiency

There once was an illness called pica in which children developed an unusual craving for dirt. Many treatments were tried, including placing cuffs on the children's wrists with strings attached to their belts so they couldn't reach their mouths. One day a pediatrician noticed that children with pica appeared pale. Comparative blood studies revealed that all of the dirt-eating children demonstrated an iron deficiency anemia. When iron was added to their diet, the pica stopped. This raises some interesting questions about unusual cravings for food that many weight-strugglers have. Is it possible that there is an unconscious attempt to seek out some missing element that their body craves? Is it possible that with increased refining of food we have eliminated some of the most nutritious parts of it, thereby inducing uncontrollable cravings for that which has been taken away?

More Recent Scientific Studies

In recent years, there has been a growing interest in studying appetite control mechanisms. Valuable research was done by the Wurtmans at Massachusetts Institute of Technology for NASA which was interested in learning about appetite control for space travel planning. In the body, proteins are made from amino acids, one of which is tryptophan. Tryptophan is also converted into serotonin, an essential organic substance in the nervous system. Serotonin is essential to normal brain function, and an abnormal reduction in quantity results in depression. It is also involved in some unknown manner in the suppression of appetite. The Wurtmans found that when a high carbohydrate breakfast was eaten by experimental subjects who demonstrated normal tryptophan blood levels, they tended to select a high protein lunch several hours later.

Further study showed that with high carbohydrate breakfasts, there was a shift of tryptophan from the blood into brain tissues.

Within an hour, as tryptophan began to fall in the blood, serotonin was released from the brain chemistry into the bloodstream, and this corresponded with a reduced craving for sweets at the later meal.[5] The serotonin-glucose mechanism may be one of the many short-term influences on our appetite, but medical knowledge of this is most incomplete.

INSULIN RECEPTOR-SITES AND APPETITE

Among the factors that influence appetite are the genetics of the insulin receptor-sites in the cells of the body. The process, summarized by Rubenstein,[6] may sound quite technical. But a basic understanding of cellular metabolism is quite helpful for counselors who want to assist those with eating disorders; it may reduce the risk of advocating simplistic and unworkable solutions to these illnesses.

Insulin facilitates the entry of glucose into cells through the cell membranes—especially muscle, liver, fat, and brain cells. As the concentration of glucose rises in the bloodstream after a meal, the level of insulin released from the pancreas also rises in response. We now know that insulin molecules can attach themselves only to specific insulin receptor-sites in much the same way that round pegs must find round holes. When an insulin molecule attaches to a receptor-site, it is pulled toward the nucleus within the cell to create a pathway for glucose through the cell membrane. It is the cell's way of refueling.

About thirty minutes after attachment, the insulin moves through the cell membrane into the cell, and can be found nestled up against the cell nucleus. There it will stay for approximately forty-eight hours. No new insulin can attach to the cell if all the receptor sites have been used after a heavy glucose meal. When saturation has thus occurred, the cell resists further uptake of glucose and the glucose in the cell is slowly burned up but not replaced. We think that as the cellular concentration of glucose drops, hunger is stimulated. (This explains the inordinate appetite of patients with uncontrolled diabetes.) Further eating causes a rise of blood sugar, but the cells literally are starving in the midst of plenty. This explains the weight loss of diabetic patients in spite of an excessive appetite.

We find that the number of insulin receptor-sites per cell is reduced in patients from families genetically predisposed toward diabetes and obesity. Indeed, thin people may have three to five times as many insulin receptor-sites per cell as someone with an excessive appetite or who is obese. Such individuals probably cannot produce enough insulin to saturate their body's insulin receptor-sites and, therefore, the overpowering hunger of the diabetic or the obese is not experienced. Therefore, a thin counselor may not appreciate the struggle with eating disorders some of his or her counselees are having.

It is important to note that the number of insulin receptor-sites can be increased by weight loss and exercise. The control of diabetes and obesity can be improved by both of these factors. However, there appear to be genetic limitations to the increase of receptor-sites; thus people with weight problems must make long-term life-style dietary changes in order to solve their problem permanently. They must consciously reduce their consumption of simple sugars which raise insulin levels more than complex carbohydrates, proteins, and fats.

Because of this mechanism, for the person with bulimia, the greater the intake of simple sugars, the greater the craving for those sugars. For this reason, I suggest that people with a tendency toward obesity or bulimia avoid the traditional three big meals a day. Instead, I recommend more frequent small meals to avoid sudden surges of blood glucose which will provoke a massive outpouring of insulin resulting in increased cravings for food, especially sweets, later. Many clients find that by measuring a cup of trail mix or other similar food each morning and by nibbling on this throughout the day, they can avoid becoming excessively hungry. By measuring the amount there is less risk of losing control of caloric consumption.

An understanding of this process, revealed to us by scientific study, should reassure the person struggling with an eating disorder that there are real, genetic, physiologic reasons for his or her cravings. They are not simply weak-willed, morally deficient, undisciplined gluttons. They are experiencing an illness that requires treatment, not guilt-inducing condemnation and punishment.

BODY WEIGHT SET POINT

Another recent and interesting area of research has been that of the "body weight set point" as reported by Faust.[7] This concept suggests that each of us has a body weight at which our appetite is in balance. When we are near that weight, we have little excess hunger and our general health is good. Should we lose weight, our appetites increase until our weight loss is regained. If we exceed that weight, our appetites are diminished until the excess weight is lost. The body weight set point probably gives us long-term control over our weight just as the carbohydrate-serotonin mechanism contributes to short-term control.

There are many reasons why a person may veer off his or her body weight set point. Some are unknown, but others include illness, genetic tendencies, the number of fat cells in the body, exercise, and mood. For example, cancer may lower body weight set point and rapid weight loss may result. Mild and moderate depression changes body weight set point and either weight gain or weight loss is the rule rather than the exception.

With an initial modest weight gain, the fat cells in the body merely increase in size. If weight control measures are instituted at this point, it is relatively easy to drop to a previous weight. However, if the excessive eating continues, the fat cells will begin to divide and thereby multiply in number. As the number of fat cells increases, it is increasingly difficult to lose to the original set point weight. For this reason it is advisable to reduce the magnitude of weight fluctuations to not more than twenty percent of usual weight.

It is useful to share the body weight set point concept with those with both anorexia nervosa and bulimia, as most of them fear that if they give up the unhealthy practices they use to control their weight that they will gain almost without limit. As they approach their healthy body weight set point they will usually find their cravings diminish and become controllable.

CHAPTER SIX

THE EFFECTS OF STARVATION

OVER THIRTY-FIVE YEARS AGO, Ancel Keys and his colleagues at the University of Minnesota performed an interesting experiment that sheds light on how dieting may disrupt the body's ability to maintain a constant appetite and body weight set point. Their experimental model revealed a remarkable similarity between behaviors observed in individuals with anorexia nervosa and bulimia, and those who have experienced semistarvation. In the experiment, thirty-six psychologically normal, physically healthy men of normal weight volunteered to restrict their caloric intake until they had lost 25 percent of their original body weight. The subjects ate normally for three months while baseline personality factors were observed. During the subsequent three months the men were restricted to one-half their former food intake. Then for a final three months of the study, they were gradually refed. The results of the study were so striking that follow-up research was continued on the men for some time after the study formally ended.[1] An excellent review of this study is found in the *Handbook of Psychotherapy for Anorexia Nervosa and Bulimia.*[2]

During the weight-loss period, the starvation produced rather dramatic changes both physiologically and psychologically. As the men reduced their caloric intake, they developed a notable preoccupation with food, to the point they had difficulty concentrating on other activities. They spent much of the day planning how they would eat and struggling between "conflicting desires to gulp their food down ravenously or consume it slowly so that the taste and odor of each morsel would be fully appreciated."[3] They also developed compulsive characteristics such as hoarding, sometimes even of nonfood items. All of the volunteers reported increased hunger. While this was tolerated fairly well by some, others would sneak in some eating binges, similar to those present in bulimia. Later, during the regaining phase, when larger amounts of food were provided, many of the men began eating compulsively or eating more or less continuously. Sometimes they experienced an increase in hunger immediately after eating.

EMOTIONAL SYMPTOMS

Although previously considered to be emotionally healthy, nearly all experienced some deterioration and one-fifth of them developed significant emotional problems. Most noted were increases in depression, hysteria, and hypochondriasis. These patterns tended to persist even during the refeeding phase and, for a few, even after the whole experiment had been over for many months. Most of the subjects became more socially isolated and withdrawn from society at large as well as from each other, just as we observe in anorexia nervosa and in some cases of bulimia. The subjects experienced a strong reduction of sexual drive. Similarly it is now known that when a woman's body fat content drops below 18 to 20 percent, hormonal dysfunction occurs. Lowered sex drive, infertility, osteoporosis, and amenorrhea result from chronic emaciation.[4]

PHYSICAL SYMPTOMS

Physiologically the most important observation of this experiment was that in starvation, as in anorexia nervosa, the person starves all over and every organ system in the body is affected. I've described a few of the many side effects that the abnormal eating practices in anorexia nervosa and bulimia can have on the central nervous system and also the rapid deconditioning of the cardiovascular system with actual shrinkage of heart size. The volunteers in the Minnesota study also experienced this and, interestingly, the heart size did not return to normal until six months after the study ended.

Because of the shrinkage of the heart, and weakening of its function, too rapid refeeding can put an excessive strain on the cardiovascular system. In my own ignorance, before I came across the work of Powers,[5] I observed symptoms of congestive heart failure in several of my own clients. This condition is vividly described in chapter 1. To avoid this problem, refeeding should be initiated in a gradual, step-by-step manner under excellent medical supervision.

During the recovery phase of the Minnesota study, many men worried about their "flabbiness," and the tendency to put on abdominal fat. So with patients with eating disorders. There is undoubtedly some impairment of digestion in starvation due to a lack of amino acids that are needed to build the complex enzymes of the liver and pancreas. It is interesting that when starving people, including those with anorexia nervosa, are refed too rapidly or with foods not easy to digest, they often suffer bloating, nausea, and even vomiting. Every missionary who has worked with starving children knows that even full strength milk is often too much for impaired digestion and is vomited. Because of this, the severely ill anorexic patient must be refed with the simplest of foods, sometimes in small amounts at frequent intervals. I have found chicken broth, even baby food, and later yogurt are well tolerated. As recovery progresses and digestion improves one can increase to more complex foods.

In the Minnesota study, as the subjects' bodies attempted to conserve tissue, thyroid activity reduced, slowing down metabolic rates. This led to sensitivity to cold, slowed thinking, and generalized weakness.

RECOVERY FROM STARVATION

In the Minnesota study, the metabolic rates responded to the refeeding. If small refeeding increments were used the response was gradual, and the corresponding strain on the heart minimal. A large meal resulted in a large rebound in metabolic rate. This may explain partially the congestive heart failure observed under these circumstances.

Most of the men in the study gained to a rebound weight that exceeded their original weight. They did not return to their original weight until six months after the study ended. The rebound phenomenon is one of the great fears that both anorexic and bulimic clients experience. They reason that if they don't stay skinny, they'll ultimately become fat. To some extent we see that the Minnesota study substantiates this fear. For this reason I encourage the recovery to be quite slow, especially as the accepted body weight is approached. It is important to establish a maintenance nutrition plan that can be followed for a lifetime. This provides support for the positive approach of eating with a food plan rather than with the negative approach of restricting calories by dieting. This contrast is similar to that between a good financial plan which shows us how we can obtain the things we need and desire, and a budget which reminds us of all the things we can't afford to buy. The food plan, like a financial plan, must be individually selected, based on individual attributes, tastes, and needs.

In this endeavor it is also important to assist the client in establishing a safe range of weight as a goal. I have found that nearly all clients are preoccupied with a specific weight above which they panic. I point out to them that no one maintains a specific weight. Indeed, after drinking a cup of water, one's weight has increased temporarily by half a pound. If the water is accompanied by a meal another pound is temporarily added. For women especially, the fluid retention associated with the menstrual cycle can cause normal weight to fluctuate by as much as five pounds. Unless they understand the temporary nature of fluid retention, they often fear that such weight increases indicate the presence of fat rather than water.

Because the Minnesota study revealed a rather slow return

to cardiac conditioning, I encourage my clients to increase their exercise tolerance in a stepwise manner as tolerated. This not only protects their weakened heart, and makes limited calorie intake available for tissue repair; as the exercise tolerance increases, it also causes the returned weight to be in the form of muscle rather than fat. I then measure their biceps and calf muscles to follow their progress. This is useful in diverting their attention away from their waist and weight with which they are preoccupied. As they approach a healthy trim weight range, their appetite is usually abated, their preoccupation with food diminished, and the compulsive rituals are directed away from food into other better served aspects of their lives. Most of the previously anorexic patients with whom I have maintained contact have continued to be five to ten pounds below their "ideal" weight as determined by the 1983 Metropolitan Life Insurance Company tables (see Appendix 1). At these weights they would be considered a healthy trim and no longer a sickly thin.

THE CASE OF THE LONG-DISTANCE RUNNER

A high school junior who had been a long-distance runner on the track team taught me the importance of considering the metabolic effects of starvation and genetic influences on thyroid function as one attempts to treat clients with anorexia and/or bulimia. Her track coach had erroneously taught her that reduction of body fat content would increase both her speed and endurance. She made body fat reduction a goal and dropped her body fat content to less than 10 percent of her body weight. When she had accomplished this, she developed the symptoms of an eating disorder with compulsive rituals about food, and a daily binge-purge syndrome. She became preoccupied with food, developing the skills of a gourmet cook, all the while maintaining a straight A average in school. She kept compulsively accurate records of her daily food intake which indicated she was existing on four hundred to six hundred calories a day.

In spite of her low calorie consumption, for a while she continued to run several miles per day. As her weight continued to drop, her endurance began to fail, and for a period she was too ill to run at all. Throughout this time she irrationally insisted that she was able to maintain her weight and strength on her severely restricted diet. Her previous physicians did not believe that her food diary was accurate, nor did her parents.

After building a relationship with her, I too voiced my skepticism and expressed the opinion that if she could maintain her activity level and weight on the lowered caloric intake, she could do so only if her thyroid function had been impaired by the starvation. I had already reviewed the Minnesota study and knew that persons who were starving would have impaired function.

Although her thyroid functions were "normal" by laboratory test, I placed her on a small dose of thyroid hormone for a four-week test. To her surprise, her weight, which was already marginal, began to drop about two pounds a week. This sudden weight loss unsettled her, and she willingly entered an in-patient eating disorder program where her calorie intake was carefully monitored. Although she was still anxious about gaining weight, her curiosity was aroused. With the help of an endocrinology consultation, she continued the low dose of thyroid medication. She increased her caloric intake rather rapidly when she saw that, with the medication, she gained no weight on twelve-hundred calories a day. Indeed, eighteen-hundred calories per day were required for weight gain without exercise and finally twenty-four hundred calories a day were required with the return of long-distance running. After three months her weight had increased from seventy-five pounds to one hundred fifteen, and she was discharged from the hospital stabilized on continued thyroid medication. During this period we also learned of a strong family history of thyroid disorders.

It is now known that subtle thyroid disorders can cause persons with depression to be resistant to usual treatment with antidepressant medication and/or cognitive psychotherapy. Often the usual laboratory tests are inadequate to detect this problem, but a therapeutic trial with thyroid medication added can sometimes bring results when other approaches fail.

CHAPTER SEVEN

SOCIAL PERCEPTION VERSUS REALITY

DAILY WE ARE BOMBARDED WITH IMAGES of who we *should* be. Women especially are faced with conflict; they live in a society that upholds as a standard of beauty female thinness, as presented by *Vogue* magazine, television, ballerinas, and the Sears catalog. Yet this same society expects them to celebrate any special event with a banquet. Indeed, it is barely proper to decline second servings of rich desserts.

The results of this bind are frightening: 85 percent of American women are not satisfied with their body size and either have dieted, are dieting, or believe that they should be dieting.[1] Data obtained by surveys in schools,[2] college campuses,[3] supermarkets,[4] and door-to-door canvassing have indicated that between 10 and 20 percent of all women will engage in bulimia at some time during their lives, and 1 to 2 percent will experience anorexia nervosa. When it comes to body shape, a significant double standard exists. Society is much more tolerant of male fatness; perhaps a small "potbelly" is accepted as a sign of affluence and success for men, while considered a disaster for women. This makes it difficult for men to have compassion for the struggles of their wives and daughters as they battle weight.

The only objective data by which standards of body size currently can be measured are in the Metropolitan Life Insurance Company tables. These tables have been established by a scientific study of longevity. The tables give the weight range associated with the longest length of life for a given height and bone structure. There is no consideration given for current socially accepted standards for appearance. The current tables were revised upward in 1983, not to ease the struggle that people have with excess weight, but to adjust to this optimum length of life which seems to be a reasonable measure of health in a large sample of people.

In the spring of 1985, fourteen national health experts met under the sponsorship of the National Institute of Health to review data relating to obesity. That conference defined obesity as 20 percent or more above normal weight tables as determined by the Metropolitan Life Insurance Company tables. It was estimated that 34 million Americans would meet this criteria and therefore were exposed to significant risk to their health and longevity.[5] For example, high blood pressure is three times more prevalent in the obese than in people of normal weight, high blood cholesterol is about two times higher, diabetes is also three times higher. In a very large study, the American Cancer Society found that obese men, regardless of smoking habits, had a higher mortality rate from cancer of the rectum, colon, and prostate than did the nonobese. Similarly, obese females, regardless of smoking habits, had a higher mortality rate from cancer of the gall bladder, biliary passages, breasts, cervix, ovaries, and uterus.[6]

From this we see that not only does society disapprove of

being overweight for aesthetic reasons, but also for real health reasons as well. Is it any wonder that young women develop fears about their weight, and especially at the time when they naturally undergo a rapid weight gain as they develop secondary sexual characteristics in adolescence? More will be said about the resulting confusion of sexual identity in chapter 11.

As women turn to the same confused society for guidance in controlling their weight, they are faced with a confusing array of opinions presented in volumes of books, many of which are "best sellers," which supposedly adds to their authoritative pronouncements. Adding to the confusion are numerous weight-reduction programs, each with the "approach that works." The young girl, watching a parade of mothers and older sisters frantically joining in the pursuit of thinness, is undoubtedly frightened and confused. The gap between society's perception of what is beautiful, and what is really healthy, has made diet books the most numerous and popular in our bookstores; and it has made weight reduction and dieting programs multi-*billion* dollar American industries.

Perhaps the confusion is the result of the ignorance that exists about nutrition, especially the false belief that there is one program that will work for everyone. All of this points to the fact that eating disorders, from anorexia nervosa through bulimia to obesity, comprise one of the major health problems in western civilization today. If we include health problems such as famine in other cultures, problems with food comprise one of the greatest threats to the health of the entire world.

John Adams Atchley, M.D., the past president of the American Anorexia and Bulimia Association, has said that eating disorders comprise the major health problem of American women today.[7]

Before we become too pessimistic, it is also necessary to point out the resurgence of our society's interest in healthy living. Health clubs are spreading rapidly across the land and they are filled with sincere people interested in improving their health through exercise. We are insisting that our grocery stores stock less junk foods and more food consistent with good nutrition. We are smoking less, drinking less, and eating fewer sweets and fats. Instead we are eating more vegetables, more complex starches, more fish and poultry. The result of these life-style changes is a significant drop in death rates from many of the diseases associated with being overweight. There is indeed hope that we are turning away from "thin is beautiful" to "trim is beautiful" because it is healthy.

PART TWO

THE TREATMENT OF ANOREXIA NERVOSA AND BULIMIA

CHAPTER EIGHT

HELPING THE HELPER

MOST BOOKS I'VE SEEN about the therapy or counseling of specific problems focus mainly on the problem and the client who struggles against it. But as a Christian psychiatrist, I have to acknowledge Christ's direction when he told us to remove the beam from our own eye so we can see more clearly to remove the speck in someone else's eye (Matt. 7:3–5). Even the secular counselor can recognize the wisdom of Pogo when he said, "We have found the enemy and they is us!" I'm occasionally asked to do a hospital consultation for a patient with an eating disorder, and I've noticed the most common reason for such a request is the frustration of the medical staff which is angry with the seeming obstinacy of an uncooperative patient. I have, therefore, elected to include in this book a major emphasis on the necessary attributes of an effective counselor of clients with eating disorders.

An example of a major blind spot is for the counselor to see the client as the problem rather than the illness itself. If a person has cancer, it is relatively easy to have compassion for the patient and see cancer as the enemy. But with eating disorders, the patient, rather than the anorexia or bulimia, is often seen as the problem. If perceived in this manner, the patient is blamed for the problem and is seen as making bad choices and employing poor judgment. Guilt often becomes the treatment modality, either through critical attacks on the client's self-esteem, dire warnings of consequences, or actual punishment by rejection of the client.

Perfectionism is a major contributing factor to the eating disorder disease process. Because the perfectionist already feels she is bad and deserving of punishment, a critical, punitive approach plays right into the dynamic of the illness, reinforcing it. This perpetual scenario can lead to chronic illness and may even bring on the ultimate punishment of death, which the person with anorexia nervosa seems to welcome yet fear.

The importance of this chapter was driven home to me while I was working on its revision. I received a phone call from a minister, upset that a young woman with an eating disorder had attempted suicide that morning. The day before he had counseled with her and had felt it important to remind her that engaging in such self-destructive behavior was a sin, that she should confess it and repent of it to obtain the healing she claimed to desire. She had become upset and had left his office in tears. The next he heard was of her suicide attempt and he was now calling me for help and guidance. The information in this chapter is presented to reduce the risk of these situations.

Many studies in America show that when people develop emotional problems, they first turn to their ministers. In fact, about 40 percent do. Less than 30 percent generally seek psychiatric or psychological counsel.[1] If the help they seek is not forthcoming, people are apt to turn from the church and seek help elsewhere. The fact that this is indeed occurring is seen in more recent studies that show fewer people turning to ministers for psychological counsel now than in prior years.[2] It is, therefore, important that we be competent so that we draw people in trouble to the Source of life by acquiring the wisdom and knowledge necessary to guide them back to health.

MY QUEST FOR TRUTH

It has now been forty-six years since I became a Christian, and nearly twenty years since I began practicing psychiatry. For me it has been and is a wonderfully terrible, sweetly bitter, easy and difficult experience, full of victories and failures. I am continually confounded by my ignorance and amazed at my occasional insights. Sometimes I feel that God had to invent eternity just because it will take that long to complete the work he has begun with me. Thank God he is patient with me, and with his help I am gradually learning to be patient with myself.

Without God's help, I have found it impossible to live a Christian life, but I do see growth. Fairly early in my psychiatric training, I began to realize that my greatest difficulty was not with patients or their illnesses but with my thoughts, feelings, and actions concerning them. As I have floundered in my Christian walk, so too I have struggled to bring order out of the chaos of multiple psychiatric theories concerning human behavior. How does one completely understand id, ego, and superego, for example? I also experienced a great struggle attempting to integrate my religious convictions and the various psychiatric theories presented to me.

Then I came across the writings of Carl Rogers who presented the concept of a therapeutic personality. It was his conclusion that the theoretical orientation is not as important as whether the therapist possesses certain personal attributes: unconditional positive regard, genuineness, and empathy.[3] That sounded close enough to the love, honesty, and compassion advocated by Christ; I spent several years clarifying these concepts and attempting to incorporate them into my life.

LOVE

As I began to seek a definition of love, I began by looking at society and found a great deal of confusion. "Making love" had more to do with sex. Freud seemed to say that love and altruism grew out of primitive id impulses relating to sex and survival. My observations seem to support this theory to the point that all of us are born quite young, quite uninformed, and totally self-centered. The infant is concerned mainly with a full stomach and physical comfort which contribute to self-preservation. If this is allowed to continue into adult life, there will be much confusion in separating wants from needs, as self-gratification will predominate. So how can we get to love and altruism from there? Is there a love that rises above sensuality? Confusion over this issue has created real havoc in our culture where it is sometimes difficult for a father to love his daughter, or a mother her son, without feeling guilty. Certainly the client with an eating disorder needs something other than appetite gratification as a basis for love. Truly a more useful definition of love had to be found.

Next I evaluated the teachings of my past. The church commonly defines *love* as self-sacrifice, the denying of one's own needs, as the needs of other people are always more important. You may remember the principle: "Jesus, others, and you; put yourself last and spell *joy*."

Consider the case of Dr. X, a dedicated internist, highly respected in the medical and church community. He served two tours in Third World countries as a medical missionary before establishing his practice in the U.S. His patients always came first and he elevated the needs of others, including his wife and children, above his own. Suddenly his behavior became erratic. He grew dissatisfied with his profession, dropped out of his church activities, and withdrew even from members of his own family. One day he abruptly left his practice, divorced his wife, and moved to an undisclosed location. He literally succumbed under the impossible burden of self-sacrifice which he had instituted at the expense of his own well-being. Self-sacrifice in itself may not always be love and can result in the kind of bondage that destroyed this man, his family, and his career. A significant portion of my own practice consists of mothers, doctors, and ministers who have burned out in their attempt to demonstrate their love by continually sacrificing their own well-being on the altar of service to others. Perhaps giving must be balanced by receiving (Eccl. 3:1–8).

Next I tried to understand the concept of unconditional positive regard, one of the attributes Carl Rogers thought important to a counselor. My analysis of each word went like this:

Unconditional: Not limited by any condition.

Positive: Explicitly expressed, real, concentrating on what is good, hopeful, or constructive.

Regard: To look upon in a particular way, to show consideration, respect, or concern for.

Many have understood Rogers to mean that we are to "like" our clients unconditionally, for the word *like* is defined as "to take pleasure in, to have a kindly or friendly feeling toward, to *regard* with favor." I am told that Dr. Rogers has stated that his concept means more than *liking*. But the concept is sufficiently vague, at least to me, to cause some uncertainty and confusion. Distinguishing the differences between *loving* and *liking* is very important; many people come to me for marriage counseling because they are in conflict and no longer like each other. Many interpret this to mean that they no longer love each other, and think divorce is their answer. If another, clearer concept of love could be found perhaps such marriages could be saved. Likewise, most clients with eating disorders do not like themselves, and cannot be persuaded to do so. Another concept of love is necessary for them also, if they are to recover their health.

Love As Mutual Concern

Only when I came across the writings of Harry Stack Sullivan did I find a definition of love that seemed workable for me. Sullivan wrote that *love may be defined as a condition that exists when another person's well-being and security are as important as your own.*[4]

This immediately resonated deep within me, for it sounded quite similar to Christ's statement that we should love our neighbor *as* we love ourselves (Matt. 19:19). I also noticed that Sullivan defined love not as a mere feeling, but as a condition that could be created by appropriate choices.

A clear definition is extremely helpful in that it gives a standard by which we may check our own behavior. Sullivan's concept of love forces us to examine what the real needs of others are by taking a closer look at our own. The Bible says that giving a cup of cold water in Christ's name is an act of love. But is giving a cup of water to a person drowning in the lake still an act of love? I think not! An act of love must be related to real need. After discovering the needs of others and placing them on a level with our own needs, a condition of love begins to exist. It is a condition resulting from conscious decisions often complemented and confirmed by emotions.

Let me illustrate love in this context: Imagine a husband and wife stranded on a desert island negotiating over their last loaf of bread. The man could nobly offer his portion to his wife as a last act of self-sacrifice before the pangs of starvation eventually extinguish their lives. Or the loaf could be equally divided between them in a perfectly equitable distribution of their last meal, thereby extending both of their lives a bit longer. Yet on further evaluation of the needs and conditions, another solution may develop. The husband might consume the entire loaf with the understanding that the nourishment will enable him to go hunt for game which would maintain the survival of them both. If, on the other hand, grain was available and the wife possessed bread-making skills, it would be more loving for her to consume the remaining loaf giving her the strength to prepare the vital substance of survival. No one loving solution will solve all problems. The solution selected will vary depending on the conditions under which the problem or conflict developed. It is my belief that *every* problem has a solution that is fair to all people involved in the problem. When that solution is found with the help of love defined as mutual concern, true healing is the *inevitable* result.

We Are Born Selfish

The newborn child does not consider the need for mother's rest when he or she cries with hunger in the middle of the night. As I see it, unless a child encounters a relationship in which mutual concern is taught, he or she will continue to live in self-centered ways. John understood this when he wrote, "We love him, because he first loved us" (1 John 4:19 KJV). Psychologists tell us now that modeling is the most important determinant of human behavior. Is this concept not what Christ also confirmed when he said, "Whatever you desire that others

would do to and for you, even so do you also to and for them
. . ." (Matt. 7:12)?

We do tend to do to others what's been done to us and I
believe God created this pattern as an efficient mechanism for
learning. It would have worked well had error not crept in,
resulting in unloving behavior which we learn by example just
as we learn loving behavior. The monkey-see, monkey-do adage
really is true. For this reason it is difficult to return good for
evil. To correct the error, Jesus pointed us back to the Source
of love and stated we must find it there and pass it on from
individual to individual when he said, "I have loved you [just]
as the Father has loved Me; . . . love one another [just] as I
have loved you" (John 15:9, 12). With this process we can overcome evil with good for only through the enabling grace of
God are we able to love others who are treating us unkindly.
Christ said it is no great skill to be kind to those who are kind
to us; even tax collectors are able to do that (Matt. 5:46). We
are directed to be channels of God's love to others who are
unloving even when in our own strength we cannot. It requires
love of this quality to bring healing to those who suffer from
eating disorders. Imagine what such a person would do if she
truly learned to care about herself; would she not take care of
that which she had learned to value, as we had first valued
her?

A clear illustration of this is found in Corrie ten Boom's book,
The Hiding Place. Corrie had the incredible experience of meeting one of the prison guards who had mistreated her and her
sister Betsie in the concentration camp. She was in Germany
after the war and was speaking on the theme of forgiveness.
After the message, the guard got in line to speak with Corrie,
and she recognized him. When he reached her, the guard told
her that he had become a Christian and that he had hoped for
the opportunity of asking forgiveness from some of those he
had abused. "Will you please forgive me, Fraulein," he asked.
Corrie said that she did not think she could do it, but that in
prayer she was reminded of Romans 5:5—"the love of God
has been poured out in our hearts by the Holy Spirit who was
given to us" (NKJV). Confessing her inability to love the man,
but being willing to be a channel of God's love if he could

work such a miracle in her heart, she reached out her hand to grasp his. To her surprise, as their hands made contact she felt a powerful surge of God's love flow through her to him. At that moment, healing came to them both.[5]

Love of this quality, love that is unconditional, is essential to bring healing to those who struggle with eating disorders. It is essential that we not just do loving acts with or for the counselee, but that we become loving people. *As we are filled with God's love, our actions will flow from a new loving nature so that we will not present just a cloak of love attempting to cover an unloving heart.*

TRUTH

Carl Rogers's second attribute of the therapeutic personality is genuineness. My dictionary says it means "realness or honesty." Most young children, although selfish, are basically honest, sometimes to the point of embarrassment of their parents. "Out of the mouth of babes . . . !" By being exposed to a harsh and punitive world, most children have learned, by age six, to engage in all the sneaky deceptions that adults and peers can teach them. Because the price to pay for honesty is so high, we learn to protect ourselves by lying. I was fascinated to learn that the word *martyr* comes from a Greek word *martus*, meaning "witness" or "one who tells the truth." Even now I struggle to have the courage to tell the truth for I have at times been ridiculed and rejected for being honest. Although parts of this book may not meet with the reader's approval, and may not be popular, I must tell what, in my experience, has been helpful to those who battle against anorexia nervosa and bulimia.

Reducing the Pain of Truth

Another difficulty with honesty is that hearing the truth can be painful. Indeed, truth not tempered with love can be very cruel, and love without an accompanying honesty can hardly be called love. In his book *Caring Enough to Confront*, David Augsburger says, "Love me enough to tell me the truth!"[6] To be useful in counseling, all truth must be run through the sieve of noncondemning love as it is expressed. Truth told in love will penetrate to the very heart, whereas truth spoken with condemnation will often be met with an impenetrable wall of defensiveness and denial. Undoubtedly this is why Christ proscribed condemnation (Matt. 7:1) and stated that his mission to earth was to save the world from it: "For God did not send the Son into the world in order to judge—to reject, to condemn, to pass sentence on—the world; but that the world might find salvation and be made safe and sound through Him" (John 3:17). This was specifically illustrated in his statement to the woman accused of adultery: "I do not condemn you either. Go on your way, and from now on sin no more" (John 8:11).

As a Man Thinks

As I continued to study the value of honesty and truth, I came across the cognitive school of psychiatry. Its pioneers include Albert Ellis,[7] Aaron Beck,[8] and David Burns.[9] The fundamental principle of this school is that our mental concepts determine our feelings and actions. The theory states that illness may be the result of false beliefs, termed *cognitive distortions*. Therapy is aimed at identifying the false belief and replacing it with truth.

There is nothing new about this principle. It is simply a restatement of the proverb: "As he thinks in his heart, so is he" (Prov. 23:7 NKJV). Doesn't the therapy sound like, "Be transformed by the renewing of your mind" (Rom. 12:2 NKJV), and, "you shall know the truth, and the truth shall make you free" (John 8:32 NKJV)?

To effectively use truth in counseling, it is necessary to have truth to share, so we do not merely replace one set of false beliefs with another. To help anyone with an illness such as anorexia nervosa or bulimia, it is vitally important to become knowledgeable about the intricacies of the illness. Love alone may not be enough. In his excellent book *Treating and Overcoming Anorexia Nervosa*, Steve Levenkron describes the authoritative, nurturant position of the counselor necessary for recovery.[10]

For the counselor to become authoritative, study is required. If we truly care about people we will take the time to seek out the knowledge and truth necessary to free them from their problem. As we have seen, parts of this book contain some

71

technical medical information. If you wish to counsel someone with an eating disorder, it may be necessary to acknowledge your ignorance and to seek out someone medically trained who can either take responsibility for the medical aspects of the illness or explain these issues sufficiently to keep the search for recovery on a straight path.

In like manner, the physician, preoccupied with medical concerns, may need to admit his or her lack of ability to love the patient unconditionally, especially when the patient seems uncooperative with the treatment. The physician may need to seek out the ability of the pastoral counselor to bring healing to this part of the problem.

In the area of eating disorders, the illnesses must be seen as complex problems with genetic, physical, intrapsychic, interpersonal, societal, and spiritual components. As most clients with eating disorders are bright and active, they are usually quite well-read and will soon detect gaps of knowledge in a counselor. If the gaps are too large and glaring, therapy will end as trust and respect are lost. This does not require that the counselor know all; it does require that he or she not cover the lack of knowledge and mislead the client into believing that she is hopeless. It is obviously better to admit one's deficiency and work with the client in seeking out accurate information.

Counselors, as well as parents, sometimes pretend they know all the answers to all the questions so that their respective clients and children will respect them for their great knowledge. This unhealthy approach is an example of a false belief that will certainly erode respect and have devastating consequences for the client. *To know that one does not know may indeed be a beginning of wisdom.* Solomon said, "Only God can see everything, and even the wisest man who says he knows everything, doesn't" (Eccl. 8:17 TLB).

As we gather truth we must weigh it and examine it. "Test and prove all things [until you can recognize] what is good; [to that] hold fast," says 1 Thessalonians 5:21. Are not secular scientists using this approach in their data-based experiments? The wise counselor will submit to reality and place his or her pet but false theory aside, while holding fast to the truth.

COMPASSION

Often the most difficult and yet necessary attribute of the therapeutic personality is that of empathy. Empathy is defined as the entrance into the feeling or spirit of another, and includes a perception of thoughts as well as feelings. It would be more comprehensive than compassion which is defined as a sympathetic emotion created by the misfortune of another accompanied by a desire to help. The concept I prefer embraces both of these words and I have found no one word sufficient to combine them into one idea, thus I use them both interchangeably, hoping that a little of each will be communicated.

Out of empathy and compassion comes the bonding between human beings, and this bonding undermines the feeling of aloneness that people who are ill often feel as they struggle against their disease. Unless empathy begins and grows into compassion, the therapeutic alliance rarely takes place.

Many patients in the hospital are surrounded by tender, loving care yet still report feeling alone due to a lack of genuine empathy and compassion in the staff, their family, and friends. A common complaint that I hear from my clients with eating disorders is that no one understands the nature or intensity of their struggles.

The apostle Paul instructed us to rejoice with others who rejoice, to weep with others who mourn (Rom. 12:15), and to bear one another's burdens (Gal. 6:2). Jesus' life was a model of empathy and he instructed us to take up his cross and follow him (Matt. 16:24). How can we bear others' burdens if we have not tasted of their pain? Perhaps this is why so many patients require support from others who are struggling or have struggled against the same problem. This is one secret of the success of Alcoholics Anonymous and other self-help groups. Indeed, Paul wrote, "Blessed [be] the God and Father of our Lord Jesus Christ, the Father of sympathy (pity and mercies) and the God [Who is the Source] of every consolation and comfort and encouragement; Who consoles and comforts and encourages us in every trouble (calamity and affliction), so that we may also be able to console (comfort and encourage) those who are in any kind of trouble or distress, with the consolation (comfort and encouragement) with which we ourselves are consoled and comforted and encouraged by God. . . . But if we are troubled (afflicted and distressed), it is for your comfort (consolation and encouragement) and [for your] salvation; and if we are comforted (consoled and encouraged), it is for your comfort and consolation and encouragement, which work [in you when you] patiently endure the same evils (misfortunes and calamities) that we also suffer and undergo" (2 Cor. 1:3, 4, 6).

On occasion I have wept with my clients as they have experienced pain and disappointments too great to express verbally. I remember working through the grief of separation with one of my clients whose family was moving to a faraway city before she was done with her therapy. In the last session she emotionally exclaimed, "Dr. Vath, will you forget me when I am gone?"

At that instant we simultaneously burst into tears and neither could talk for five minutes. Later when we left the office, I mentioned to her mother, in the waiting room, that we were having a hard time saying good-bye. She quickly responded, "I know, Jennifer is really struggling with that." Immediately I said, "No, *we* are having a hard time saying good-bye." When she reads this she'll know I've not forgotten!

It is often difficult for us to be empathetic because we assume that we know how another feels in a given situation. When anyone hears, "I know what you must feel," his or her immediate response is often doubt and disbelief. Why? Because our emotional responses to stimuli are learned. For example, if five accountants were fired from their jobs, one might respond with violent anger, wanting to bodily harm the employer. Another might respond with depression and suicidal thoughts, feeling that life is only one calamity after another. A third might respond with worry and fear, pacing the floor and staring at the ceiling night after sleepless night. A fourth might respond with internalized frustration, developing ulcers or high blood pressure. The fifth might respond with collaborative problem solving, evaluating resources, and sending out résumés. Each person would feel his or her emotional response was the natural one, as it was the one learned in childhood. Yet the outside observer can see that each response is different and can be unlearned— in the direction, one would hope, of the fifth response which is the healthiest of the lot.

A primary step in developing empathy is realizing that we must not assume how another thinks or feels, but that we must allow the thoughts and feelings to be expressed in an atmosphere of love and commitment. Only when we truly know how another thinks and feels, and when the other validates the accuracy of our perception, empathy and compassion exist. Assumptions about another person's thoughts and feelings are sure to kill empathy and compassion.

Another reason empathy is difficult to experience is that our language tends to be either attackingly aggressive or defensively evasive. We have learned to focus on the error of the other, rather than reveal our own thoughts and feelings in the circumstance. It is easier to say, "You make me sick!" than, "I feel upset when I think I have been treated unfairly." This leads to defending ourselves from attack rather than sharing our burdens with others. If I can't or don't tell you how I feel, how can you know of my burden? When you know of my burden you will be able to follow Paul's advice to bear one another's burden, for in God's economy a burden shared is less than one-half as heavy and the reduced burden can allow healing to occur.

GETTING IT TOGETHER

These three learnable attributes—love, honesty, and compassion—are essential if we are to minister to others who are ill. Like the answer to the question, "Which is the most important leg of a three-legged stool?" all three are equally important. These skills work together to bring about the powerful impact of healing. Just as a cake is created with certain essential ingredients, the attributes of love, honesty, and compassion are essential to the personality of a healer. Without all three, we are apt to do more harm than good, being like the blind who lead the blind.

On the other hand, Christ stated that love is the greatest of all virtues (Matt. 22:39, 40) and implied that from love all other virtues flow. Without love, truth becomes unnecessary and compassion impossible, for unless a client believes you truly care she will not tell you who she is. Only if she believes that you truly care and understand will she accept and incorporate into her life any truths that you have to share with her.

How can you acquire these therapeutic attributes? By recognizing that you are somewhat deficient in them and by dedicating your life to becoming more loving, honest, and compassionate. What greater epitaph could be on your tombstone than "Here lies a loving, honest, and compassionate person"? Perhaps this is what Christ meant when he said, "But seek . . . first of all, His kingdom, and His righteousness [His way of doing and being right], and then all these things taken together will be given you besides" (Matt. 6:33).

Is There a Christian School of Psychiatry?

I am often asked what school of psychiatry I belong to. Although it is technically true to say that I am eclectic in my therapy, the school of psychiatry I readily identify with is found in Galatians, chapter 6. Here it is, as stated in The Amplified Bible:

Brethren, if any person is overtaken in misconduct or sin of any sort, you who are spiritual—who are responsive to and controlled by the Spirit—should set him right and restore him and reinstate him, without any sense of superiority and with all gentleness, keeping an attentive eye on yourself, lest you should be tempted also.

Bear (endure, carry) one another's burdens and troublesome moral faults, and in this way fulfill and observe perfectly the law of Christ, the Messiah, and complete what is lacking in [your obedience to it]. For if any person thinks himself to be somebody [too important to condescend to shoulder another's load], when he is nobody [of superiority except in his own estimation], he deceives and deludes and cheats himself.

But let every person carefully scrutinize and examine and test his own conduct and his own work. He can then have the personal satisfaction and joy of doing something commendable [in itself alone] without [resorting to] boastful comparison with his neighbor. For every person will have to bear [be equal to understanding and calmly receive] his own (little) load [of oppressive faults]. Let him who receives instruction in the Word [of

God] share all good things with his teacher—contributing to his support.

Do not be deceived and deluded and misled; God will not allow Himself to be sneered at—scorned, disdained or mocked [by mere pretensions or professions, or His precepts being set aside].—He inevitably deludes himself who attempts to delude God. For whatever a man sows, that and that only is what he will reap. For he who sows to his own flesh (lower nature, sensuality) will from the flesh reap decay and ruin and destruction; but he who sows to the Spirit will from the Spirit reap life eternal.

And let us not lose heart and grow weary and faint in acting nobly and doing right, for in due time and at the appointed season we shall reap, if we do not loosen and relax our courage and faint. So then, as occasion and opportunity open to us, let us do good (morally) to all people [not only being useful or profitable to them, but also doing what is for their spiritual good and advantage]. Be mindful to be a blessing, especially to those of the household of faith—those who belong to God's family with you, the believers (6:1–10).

Isn't this statement clear? All the ingredients of cognitive-behavioral therapy are present. The goal of restoration is clear. The approach both gentle and humble, with cautions concerning the need to keep an eye on one's self. The unchanging reality of cause and effect is the measuring stick by which appropriate beliefs, feelings, and behavior are determined. Finally, there is the encouraging statement that we will attain the goal of restoration if we have the patience and persistence.

CHAPTER NINE

THE BEST LITTLE GIRL IN THE WORLD
The Perfectionism Factor

As I have pointed out previously, eating disorders are the result of complex behaviors made up of many factors. Therapeutic success seems to be related to the ability to identify those factors in each individual, both to the degree and the manner in which they are present, and then to design and execute a specific treatment plan for each of the factors. The items that I noted in chapter 2 are the subjects of the next seven chapters. I discuss them in the order that came to me, but in therapy the issues may present themselves in a different sequence and may be resolved in an order still different from that in which they are uncovered. Often it is necessary to work on several issues simultaneously.

Perfectionism leads individuals to unrealistic and therefore unattainable expectations of themselves. Although this mindset is not limited to those with eating disorders, in my opinion it is one of the major root causes of anorexia nervosa and bulimia. These individuals have such extreme rules and definitions by which they measure themselves that nearly everything they attempt becomes a failure, leading to exquisite torment as the feelings of inadequacy and worthlessness grow. Each unreasonable expectation is based on a false belief, or, as the cognitive therapist would prefer to label them, "cognitive distortion." And each must be identified and then corrected by demonstrating the irrational and illogical aspects of the client's thoughts, feelings, and actions.

Many times the patient is more aware of the feeling and the actions that result from an idea than she is of the idea itself. The idea is often so fleeting or so unconscious that it takes some effort on the part of the counselor to bring it to her conscious attention. As you work with a patient, her belief system gradually becomes more apparent to you and, more importantly, to her. Drawing out root issues is relatively easy for a skilled observer who has removed some of the beams from his or her own eyes. The greater difficulty comes in persuading the perfectionist that some of her belief systems are faulty. For even though her belief system is not working very well, the perfectionist often feels that it is "perfect."

CONDITIONAL LOVE

What causes perfectionism? One answer is the false idea that I find present in every person with an eating disorder: "I won't be loved unless I am perfect."

This obviously comes from a society in which value is determined by performance and achievement as measured by salary and bank accounts, by popularity and social position, by other people's opinions of you including how much anger and punishment you receive for your mistakes, and your grade point in school, to name a few. Such conditional love is rampant in the world, but has no place in the relationship between therapist and patient or minister and wounded soul. Indeed, Cherry Boone O'Neill said that ultimately her healing from anorexia and bulimia came when she started to believe that she was lovable even with her illness. Even with her failures and her sins, she was still valued and cared for unconditionally by her God who went so far as to number the very hairs on her head.[1]

Use Bible Stories to Challenge Perfectionism

The whole flow of the Bible is the story of God working mightily through imperfect men and women such as Abraham, who lied to Pharaoh saying that his wife was indeed his sister. Abraham's lack of faith is seen in his attempt to speed God's plan by fathering a child by his handmaiden, Hagar, sowing seeds of the Arab/Israeli conflict to the present day. Yet his faith was counted unto him as righteousness.

We also see the impetuous Moses who had a hot temper that surfaced again and again. When he was young, he killed an Egyptian. He smashed the stone tablets and later, while leading the children of Israel across the wilderness, he smote the rock. Yet he was a man who walked and talked with God.

We see the errors of David, a man after God's own heart who failed first by seducing Bathsheba, and second by killing Uriah her husband in an attempt to hide his first sin. We see David's rebellion as he took a census in spite of God's warning that he should count on God's strength in battle rather than on the size of his nation. In many respects Saul was a better king than David, but when the prophet Samuel came to correct him Saul would harden his heart, becoming more and more obstinate in his sin. David, however, continually humbled himself, confessing and repenting of his sin in a visible manner for all the nation to see. All this clearly explains that God's love of us and our salvation are not dependent on our goodness but on God's unconditional love for us with our failures and our sins.

Rahab, a prostitute, believing God was with the children of Israel, risked her life to help Joshua's spies. Her act of faith not only saved her life, but also allowed her to become a part of Christ's lineage.

Recall the strong man of God, Elijah. He literally prayed fire from heaven to consume his sacrifice and altar. And yet immediately afterward, he ran and hid from the angry queen.

Fearing for his life, he said that he might as well lie down and die. But God sent a messenger to strengthen and comfort Elijah and to challenge him with the truth that he was not the only prophet left in Israel and that because of God's help he had nothing to fear.

The New Testament tells the story of Peter and his friends, James and John, called "sons of thunder" because of their impulsive bent. Peter was willing to take on the soldiers of the Sanhedrin when he alone took out his sword and single-handedly began to defend Christ. A few hours later, he just as impulsively denied that he even knew Christ, only to repent and weep bitterly as he remembered the prophecy Christ had made about his actions.

Illustration after illustration make it obvious that the message of the entire Bible is that our faith in God is what is counted unto righteousness; God's love of us is not conditional upon our performance or our goodness; God loves us not in spite of our faults, sins, and errors; he loves us with them. This same attitude must be present in the therapist when working with someone with a self-destructive eating disorder, for only with such an attitude can the basic belief that love is conditional upon perfection be corrected.

I remember when a bulimic patient who had been raised in a very legalistic church reported a recurrent nightmare: She was walking a narrow high beam in a large cathedral-like building. The beam was two hundred feet in the air, towering above the floor which was covered with snakes and alligators. She had to walk the whole length of the building on the narrow beam and she knew the slightest slip would plunge her to a horrible death. She felt frozen with fear, unable to go forward or back. She was tempted to jump or fall just to end the torment.

It was not difficult for us to decipher the symbolic meaning of this dream and its relationship to her need to be perfect. The impasse of the eating disorder was also clear. The slightest slip would lead to death. Losing weight would lead to physical death, gaining weight would lead to loss of control and to a social and psychological death. Physical death seemed preferable and, although frightening, began to be welcomed. It takes a great deal of support and encouragement for such a person to risk taking a small step toward health when the dangers seem so great.

Use Doctrine to Challenge Conditional Love

If clients are Christian believers, I point them to the Scriptures that state that our salvation is "not because of works . . . lest any man should boast" (Eph. 2:9); that "all our righteousness are as filthy rags" (Isa. 64:6); that "He saved us, not because of any works of righteousness that we had done, but because of His own pity and mercy, by [the] cleansing (bath) of the new birth (regeneration) and the renewing of the Holy Spirit" (Titus 3:5). Further, Romans 4:1–8 states:

> [But] if so, what shall we say about Abraham, our forefather humanly speaking? (How does it affect his position, and what was gained by him?) For if Abraham was justified (that is, established as just by acquittal from guilt) by good works [that he did, then] he has grounds for boasting. But not before God! For what does the Scripture say? Abraham believed (trusted in) God, and it was credited to his account as righteousness— right living and right standing with God. [Gen. 15:6] Now to a laborer, his wages are not counted as a favor or a gift, but as an obligation—something owed to him. But to one who not working [by Law] trusts (believes fully) in Him Who justifies the godly, his faith is credited to him as righteousness—the standing acceptable to God. Thus David congratulates the man and pronounces a blessing on him to whom God credits righteousness apart from the works he does: Blessed and happy and to be envied are those whose iniquities are forgiven and whose sins are covered up and completely buried. Blessed and happy and to be envied is the person of whose sin the Lord will take no account nor reckon it against him (Ps. 32:1, 2).

On the other hand, some clients are quick to point out the Scriptures that seem to advocate the necessity of works in the Christian life. "Faith by itself, if it does not have works, is dead" (James 2:17 NKJV). "Was not Abraham our father justified by works . . .?" (James 2:21 NKJV). And so we seem to be confronted with a paradox that shows salvation is not by works and yet works are necessary for salvation. I explain that works can be put on as an outer garment, a mere cloak of righteousness, but whenever one does this out of a sense of duty, the works become meaningless. The solution to the paradox is that we must focus on being rather than doing.

If indeed I've become a loving person, the acts of love will flow from my loving nature and not be merely that cloak of righteousness to which Christ referred (Matt. 23:27–29). James is saying that if there are no works, the being (essence of a Christian personality) is questionable for they must go hand in hand. He concludes his dissertation with, "For as the human body apart from the spirit is lifeless, so faith apart from [its] works of obedience is also dead" (James 2:26), showing that one cannot separate a healthy Christian's faith from his or her works. Although the Pharisee works to earn love, the loving Christian works as an expression of his loving nature. It is my opinion, that the faith to which James refers is the faith in God's Word as truth, faith in God who loves us unconditionally, faith in God's work, and "while we were still sinners Christ, the Messiah, the Anointed One, died for us" (Rom. 5:8).

Use History to Challenge Conditional Love

It is somewhat more difficult to persuade a nonbeliever that striving for perfection doesn't earn or guarantee love. Why? Because the results or fruits of hard work are often enormous. After all, "the early bird gets the worm" and "early to bed, early to rise, makes a man healthy, wealthy, and wise." Such individuals have a superficial belief that the end of work is wealth; from wealth comes admiration, respect, love, joy and power. Fortunately many life stories have demonstrated the fallacy of this belief.

The biography of John D. Rockefeller is the story of a young man who drove himself to accumulate fame and fortune. Yet at age fifty he was a sick man who had difficulty digesting even simple foods. Although he had made himself one of the world's wealthiest men, he had become one of the most hated men in America, where laws had been passed specifically against him and his enterprises. Only then did he see the error of his ways and change his philosophy. He funded the University of Chicago and the Rockefeller Foundation as he began openly to give back to the world from his abundance. Although he continued to be somewhat hypochondriacal until his death at the ripe age of ninety-eight, he gained much respect and admiration in his later years.[2]

The tragic deaths of movie stars, such as Marilyn Monroe, William Holden, and Elvis Presley, to name just a few, also demonstrate that fame and fortune can become a disappointing burden rather than a blessing.

Use Real-life Examples to Challenge Conditional Love

After presenting such concrete examples, I turn my attention to personal life experience of the client. I might ask the perfectionist, often a good student, "How many people have come to love you because you get straight As?" She often reports that "eggheads" are indeed often seen as weird by the fun-loving B- and C-students. She may also see that, in spite of her best efforts, there is always something that someone can find fault with in her. This adds one more piece of evidence that I can use to refute her belief that success brings love. It allows us to begin to replace that belief with the truth that it is love that brings success.

Use Yourself to Challenge Conditional Love

One of the most powerful tools I use in addressing conditional love that contributes to perfectionism is to acknowledge in a nondefensive way my own errors, failures, and weaknesses. When my heritage of legalistic fundamentalism, German ancestry, and Air Force officer training resulted in a forceful, critical, controlling personality, I nearly destroyed myself and my family. I encounter patients and their families who share some of these traits, and when I do I am able to relate my experiences to them without shame or blame while pointing out the reality of my transformation as I finally sought God's way rather than my own. Now I am able to enjoy the wonderful blessings that God has promised when we live his way.

One experience that is particularly helpful to share and which was a major turning point in my life occurred when my oldest daughter was about eight years old. I had been watching the news on TV when my wife called me for supper. My daughter, wanting to be helpful, ran in and turned off the TV. Because I had not given her permission, I was enraged and swatted her. Later that night she awakened screaming in terror, saying "a bear was getting me"! When I got up to comfort her, it was as though God were talking to me as the question entered my mind, "Who do you think the bear is?" And another question came: "Do you want her to be afraid of you, or do you want her to love and respect you?" I responded, "What kind of choice is that? Of course, I want her love and respect!" Then came the question, "What will you have to change in your life in order for that to happen?" I knew I had to change. Over the ensuing years I have given up my temper and have learned to truly love and care for my family; and now my family does love and respect me.

Another example that is useful is to point out that my glasses kept me from my youthful dream of becoming a fighter pilot with the Air Force. My poor eyesight may have saved my life. Still, I did have a successful ten-year military career, first as a meteorologist and later as a physician. Also, although my one-hundred, fifty-five pound frame has prevented me from becoming a fullback for the Seattle Seahawks, I do have a very fulfilling life. Although I have weaknesses, God has given me other strengths that have been more than enough, for "My strength is made perfect in weakness" (2 Cor. 12:9 KJV). I can, therefore, love and care for myself with my failures and my weaknesses, for God loves me unconditionally. And who's to argue with him?

CRITICISM AS A CAUSE OF PERFECTIONISM

Another false belief related to perfectionism is that being the object of anger or criticism is absolutely intolerable. When we are attacked we feel like giving up and running away, or like counter-attacking and giving back what we are receiving.

Christ said, "Woe to (alas for) you when everyone speaks fairly and handsomely of you . . ." (Luke 6:26). He also said in Matthew 5:11, 12, "Blessed . . . are you when people revile you and persecute you and say all kinds of evil things against you falsely on My account. Be glad and supremely joyful, for your reward in heaven is great . . . for in this same way people persecuted the prophets who were before you."

Steve Levenkron feels that the anorexic is often a person of great self-sacrifice, attracting much of the irritability and criticism of a depressed family onto herself.[3] By being the scapegoat, she attempts to maintain the stability of the family. The problem is that the anorexic has neither the strength nor the wisdom to understand this dynamic. Therefore, because her perfectionism makes criticism intolerable, she literally lays down her life for her family.

Positive Aspects of Criticism

It is important to remind the client that wise people love correction, that anger or disapproval should be considered objectively and weighed. Any truth in the disapproval can be gleaned and used beneficially but should not be used as a form of self-punishment or as a source of ammunition for retaliation. Here again the examples of Abraham, Moses, Rahab, Elijah, David, and Peter can be used as a healthy response to disapproval of or anger aimed at one's error. Each of these people responded wisely to God's discipline. Try teaching the client to translate the angry language of a correcting society into the clear issues of the conflict that needs to be resolved so that solutions can be found and change can result.

For example, if a client says, "I hate my parents!" I will ask, "What is it about them that you dislike so strongly?" When the reply is, "They never listen to me!" I respond, "We need to find a way to speak to them in ways they can hear. Perhaps a family session will help us uncover why communication is blocked between you and them."

When parents rely on anger and criticism to manipulate and correct behavior, children can get so busy defending themselves from the anger and criticism, that they don't see the original issue. When angry emotion comes in, reason and clarity can go out the window. When such a family pattern has developed, clarification and correction are necessary objectives of therapy. Parents must be shown that change is "Not by might, nor by power, but by my Spirit, saith the Lord of hosts" (Zech. 4:6 KJV). We must remind them that truth is what sets people free, not the fear of anger, which often only drives behavior underground. Anger reinforces the perfectionist's striving for that perfect life that is above reproach, that life that hopes to avoid the physical and emotional pain that results from punitive anger.

The problem is that there is no behavior that at some time will not displease others. If I become a Republican, my Democratic friends think I've lost my mind; if I become a Democrat, my Republican friends criticize, condemn and reject me; if I become an Independent, both Democratic and Republican friends call me wishy-washy, which illustrates that there is no place to hide from any and all criticism. Similarly, the anorexic and bulimic will never attain the perfect life they so actively seek.

I often observe that a client is so used to thinking in an angry, critical, and self-condemning manner herself, that even simple observations are translated into criticism. For example, one day one of my clients walked into my office and burst into tears. When I calmly acknowledged that she was crying, she angrily responded, "Oh Doctor Vath, there you go criticizing me too!" After a minute of quiet contemplation, I responded, "I am puzzled that you would hear a criticism in my simple observation of your tears." This led to an exploration of her reaction: Tears had never been acceptable in her family and she was continually ridiculed and condemned for her crying. Eventually when well-meaning people noticed her emotional distress and reached out to her, she reacted as if they were rejecting her, thereby cutting herself off from the offered healing comfort. As she became aware of this tendency, she began to welcome the acknowledgment of her distress. She could then incorporate the compassionate love that was already available to her. This led to her eventual recovery.

Learning to React Positively to Criticism

It is important to help individuals who are afraid of anger and disapproval gradually to become desensitized. All too often we counsel that they should avoid being around angry people rather than that they should learn to respond to anger skillfully and nondefensively. Years ago if someone had said to me, "I would like to attend your church, but there are too many hypocrites in it," I would have responded defensively. In a counter-attack, I would have said, "You infidel, how dare you point your finger at a good person like myself?" But now I have found that such responses only serve to alienate me from others. I now know that it is more accurate and helpful to say, "I cannot speak for the church, but I know that I fall far short of the standards of perfection to which I ascribe. If you notice such inconsistencies, please call them to my attention. Your observations could help me in my personal growth."

As a young parent, I was incensed if my children found fault with my decisions, but I have learned that many of my decisions are faulty. Now when my children question how I arrive at a decision, I admire their courage and honesty, and I give their observations thoughtful consideration. I have learned that my children respect me for this receptive attitude because of its honesty. Conversely, when I tried to win their respect by insisting that I was right all the time, I eventually lost their respect. Furthermore, when I listen to them, they listen to me, and we all grow in wisdom.

When teaching clients to deal with criticism, I share three major steps.

Develop Empathy with the Accuser. It is essential not to focus on the rightness or wrongness of the criticism (this leads only to endless arguments), but instead to focus on what the criticism means. What is the hurt, the fear, the concern, that prompted the emotional outburst? What conflict produces such intense emotion? This focuses the attack away from the anger and on to the issues of the conflict. There is often little one can do about the other's disapproval or criticism but, if we can clarify the conflict from which the anger arises, we can usually do something to relieve the source of the tension. When building bridges, it is essential to know precisely where both sides of the river are. This is an essential use of compassion.

Disarming the Critic. If the accused shoots back, the war continues and escalates. People will tend to do to us what we do to them. It is important to find some grounds upon which the accused can honestly agree with the critic. Matthew 5:25 says that we should come to quick agreement with our adversaries. Next, can the accused find something positive in the criticism? Sometimes this may be nothing more than, "At least it will help me grow and acquire skill in handling criticism." Again, Proverbs 15:5 says, "He that regardeth reproof is prudent" (KJV), whereas Proverbs 15:10 says, "he that hateth reproof shall die" (KJV). Inviting even more criticism can even facilitate growth. When one receives criticism in this manner and accepts responsibility for his or her own actions, the accusers tend to respond in kind and look more carefully at their own actions in response. This leads us to principle number three.

Discuss and Negotiate. After identifying the source of the conflict and acknowledging her own human weakness and potential for error, the accused can then suggest alternative solutions that lead to an objective resolution of the conflict. Solutions are based on the principle of fairness and reality rather than merely winning a victory at someone else's expense.

For example, when the mother of a bulimic patient angrily exclaimed, "Our daughter is destroying the family with her enormous waste of food," I noticed the crushed, guilty look on her daughter's face. I asked the daughter if she felt her bulimia was a waste of food and she readily agreed it was, but she could not help herself. I then asked if anyone could come up with a solution to the problem and several were suggested. A lock on the refrigerator, making her move out of the house, making her pay for her own food, and punishing her by restricting her privileges (driving, shopping) were quickly offered. I then asked if there were some way of combining these suggestions into a workable plan. After much discussion the family decided to place a lock on the pantry to keep the bulk of the family food protected and to assist the daughter with her impulse control. She was given a shelf in the kitchen for her food and a weekly allowance to keep it stocked. If more funds were needed she would have to earn them. As a solution was found and the conflict resolved, positive steps in dealing with anger in time became second nature to this family as their daughter went on to recovery.

Once I was strongly criticized by a high school girl I was treating for bulimia. I had been responsible for having her committed to a psychiatric hospital after she had made a suicide attempt because she felt her bulimia was beyond control. She asked what right I had to violate her confidence and bring others into her life? How could she ever trust me again? I quickly acknowledged that I had violated her confidence and that she could not trust me to keep life-threatening secrets. In fact, she could trust me to react and *act* under those circumstances. I would rather face her anger than see her dead. She then admitted her fear that I did not care if she lived or died and she never again threatened suicide.

THE PROBLEM OF BLACK-AND-WHITE THINKING

As a result of the distortions of conditional love, the pursuit of the elusive goal of a life above reproach, and intolerance to disapproval, the perfectionistic person with an eating disorder often develops a tendency toward black-and-white thinking: "If I'm not getting straight As in school, I might as well get straight Fs." "If everybody doesn't love me, no one can love me at all." "If I can't do a job perfectly, I might as well not try." Scripture verses such as Matthew 5:48 can be used by a client to reinforce this unhealthy view of a perfect life in stark contrast to a life of failure. But this verse, "You shall be perfect, just as your Father in heaven is perfect" (NKJV), is further explained in The Amplified Bible: "You, therefore, must be perfect . . . [that is, grow into complete maturity of godliness in mind and character, having reached the proper height of virtue and integrity]." This amplification implies a process of growing toward perfection rather than living immediately in a manner unattainable in human power, strength, and cleverness. Maybe God invented eternity because he knows it will take a long time to grow to perfection.

In his book *On Guerrilla Warfare,* Chairman Mao states that in every weakness there is a strength and in every strength a weakness.[4] With that philosophy, he successfully guided the expansion of communism to many parts of the world. It sounds vaguely similar to Christ's statement, "He who finds his life will lose it, and he who loses his life for My sake will find it" (Matt. 10:39 NKJV). Chairman Mao was wrong, though, when he said that power came from the muzzle of a gun, for there is greater power in love. See Zechariah 4:6. This demonstrates that misguided men can have great truth and wisdom in one area, but be totally misguided in others. To some degree all of us fit into this pattern; thus, to think of anyone being all right or all wrong is irrational.

VATH'S RULES FOR LIVING

When challenging the blackness or whiteness of the perfectionist's thinking, I teach my counselee the four Vath rules:

1. If it's worth doing, it's worth doing even poorly.
2. Practice makes better, not perfect.
3. It is better to try and fail than to fail by not trying.
4. We should fail at half the things we try in life or we'll never know what we are capable of accomplishing.

To facilitate the incorporation of these ideas by my client, I hand them the four Vath Rules in printed form and tell them to paste them on the bathroom mirror. They are to read them daily until they truly believe them. Encounters like this make therapy more pleasant and are part of "the spoonful of sugar that makes the medicine go down."

When people first hear these rules, they usually smile, or burst into laughter. This usually means we have given them rules for their "child" to use in countering the erroneous injunctions of their "punitive parent." They begin to realize that they may never attain complete perfection in a tennis game, winning every match, and yet they recognize it still can be an enjoyable sport. In a similar vein, I remind them that learning to love and be concerned for others is worth the effort even though no one loves and cares perfectly. I also remind them that there are degrees in loving, that it too is not an all-or-nothing venture. With practice they will get better at it.

The second rule illustrates that with practice, skills improve, but never to the level of perfection. Many people spend years training for the Olympics, and yet no Olympic champion wins every race, even when he or she is the world's best.

It has been estimated that there are about one billion Christians in the world.[5] If practice made perfect, wouldn't at least one of them step forward and proclaim that he or she had attained it? After all, it takes only one white crow to prove all crows aren't black. My translation of Paul's statement in Galatians 6:5 is, "While I wait for the Perfect One to come, I'll accept a little gray in the best of us."

My third rule is important for those people who are immobilized by their fear of failure and cannot even begin their pursuit of a goal. This often results from the thought that failure is intolerable. It is helpful to trace this back to their belief that love is conditional upon success and that all failure will be punished.

In the fourth rule I illustrate that a fifty-fifty success-failure ratio adds to the excitement of living. If we play chess and you or I consistently win every game, we would both soon lose interest. Only when we're evenly matched and either success or failure is likely does the game really become exciting and challenging.

If we do not risk failure, we often elude success altogether.

When I began to get interested in treating people with eating disorders, I was told that they all have a very low rate of recovery, that they were deeply imprisoned by behavioral patterns that they were powerless to break. Right then and there I could have given up and decided not to risk failure in my professional life. But I did decide to risk. In those early years I didn't strive for success; I simply sought to be helpful. And I gradually learned enough about the illnesses to help my clients break free from many of their bonds. Eventually I attained a level of knowledge that led to success far beyond what I had dreamed possible.

When working with clients, many opportunities present themselves for the practical application of these rules. I might ask if it is worth struggling against their illness, even though they may fail. Virtually all will give some agreement to this question. Would it help to reduce binging to once a day from twice a day? Would raising blood pressure a few points by gaining a few pounds, thereby stopping fainting episodes, be useful in reducing fear? Most patients will be curious and will at least attempt these experiments even though they may fail. If the anorexic can't gain five pounds, even the gain of a pound or two is a step toward health. When the small step succeeds, practice through repetition makes further steps easier, and thus practice is proven to make better.

I recall an anorexic patient who was so afraid to get well

and leave home that she failed at every task that might lead to her emancipation from the family. We persuaded her to take a typing course at a local community college, and sure enough, twenty words a minute seemed to be the maximum rate she could attain. After she tearfully stated she was failing at this endeavor also, I reminded her that at least she was trying, and was risking failure, and that this had allowed her to experience a response from me that she might find unusual. Instead of criticizing her lack of success, I pointed to the fact that she was typing twenty words a minute, and reminded her that practice would make better even if it might take a while.

I called her attention to the reality that we live in an upside-down world where the weak and the ill are too frequently pounced upon, exploited, ridiculed, and condemned. On the other hand, the successful are envied. I pointed out to her the contrasting teachings of Christ as reported by Paul in Romans 12:15, "Rejoice with those who rejoice, and weep with those who weep" (NKJV). Thus I could be happy for her twenty-words-a-minute typing skill while responding compassionately to her profound feelings of failure.

With this new experience, she gradually increased her typing speed to fifty words a minute, and began to apply for work. Initially, she froze during the required typing tests and the sense of failure would return. Again I pointed out to her that at least she could experience a positive, comforting response to her failure. After five attempts she finally did pass a test and obtained a most satisfactory job. This was a major step in her emancipation from her family. This success gave her the hope that her anorexia could also be resolved, and with a similar, step-by-step approach, her weight returned to normal.

In a loving, empathetic environment, patients will gradually learn to live in a world that is not "black or white." As they become more comfortable with ambivalence their all-or-nothing, success-or-failure, perfectionistic attitudes will be gradually modified toward realism. You will need to comfort them through any failure and acknowledge even the smallest success.

The water in the glass of life may be either half empty or half full, depending on one's level of optimism. But in the eyes of the realist, the glass is both half empty and half full and even "with all of its sham, drudgery and broken dreams, it is still a beautiful world" (*Desiderata*).

CHANGING THE BEHAVIOR OF THE PERFECTIONIST

As my client begins to see that the belief system upon which her personality is based may be flawed and that alternative truths may be more valid, I begin focusing on behavioral changes that can confirm the validity of the changing beliefs. I encourage Christian patients to rise to the challenge of 1 Thessalonians 5:21, to test everything and hold onto that which proves to be true and good.

One young airline stewardess had been attempting to limit her weight (and thus maintain her job) with bulimic behaviors. One night, after being treated with appropriate antidepressant medication for two months and nearly ceasing the bulimic behavior, she developed a craving for Mexican food. She went out with a friend and consumed about twelve hundred calories of food. When she anxiously weighed herself the next morning, she was surprised to see that she had lost, not gained, nearly a pound. This is not uncommon early in treatment, for bulimic behaviors do cause some inefficiency of digestion and impairment of metabolic process. When she relayed this experience to me, I was able to point out that her assumptions weren't based on truth; eating does not automatically lead to immediate weight gain. This insight gave her the courage to begin to experiment flexibly with her diet. Perfect control was no longer quite so important to her.

I suggest that all clients, Christian and non-Christian alike, study the cause and effect relationship between their belief systems and their resulting feelings and behavior. I can best describe this experiment by relaying a specific example. One day I was counseling with a perfectly attired woman who didn't have a hair on her head out of place. She was complaining that there was never enough time in the day for herself; housekeeping and childcare occupied all her time and energies.

I asked a simple question, "Do you believe you shouldn't play until after all your work is done?" She said yes, that was what she had been taught as a child and the principle by which she'd lived to the present moment.

"What would you like to do if the work could be all caught up?" I asked. And she said, "Oh, I'd like just to go shopping with a friend, but there never seems to be enough time."

I suspected that her house was as neatly kept as her own person, and she readily agreed. I then asked if she would attempt the following experiment: On one day of the following week, while she was making the beds, she would leave one corner of a pillow uncovered with the bedspread folded neatly, if she preferred. She was then to call her friend, arrange for, and go on a brief trip to a local shopping mall. Throughout the morning she was to take note of her thoughts and feelings and, the following week, report them to me.

Wanting to please me perfectly, she did as was requested. When she came in, she said, "Doctor Vath, it was the most interesting experience. I couldn't get the uncovered pillow out of my mind the entire time I was at the shopping mall. It finally dawned on me. *Here I am, worrying about an uncovered pillow that no one will ever know about but myself.* I was allowing that concern to destroy the pleasure of the moment. That was the first time I could see how I had allowed the insignificant things in life to destroy my joy."

In the weeks that followed, I gently encouraged her to repeat the process, to do something pleasurable in the morning, leaving some small task undone. Eventually I asked her which of these events she was going to remember ten years from now, and gradually she began to relax and strike a balance between being an efficient, industrious wife and allowing herself the joy and pleasure of play.

I've often given a similar task to perfectionists who are so rigidly fixed that they are unwilling to try even a simple experiment previously described. In the week following a session they are to go out and waste a penny, a task that seems simple and superficial. If they come and gleefully report that they gave it away, I ask them if their gift brought the recipient pleasure. If they say they lost it, I ask them if the finding of it might have brought joy to the finder or, if it fell into the soil, did it not return to nature an essential element, copper. If they spent it on something "foolish," did it contribute to the merchant's prosperity and, therefore, his joy? What started as a simple exercise becomes much more complex when seen from a different perspective. This helps the client overcome fear of failure, for even "waste" can have benefit if one looks for it. Such an experiment is often the starting point for movement into other experiments, more relevant to the life of the client.

The "lazy" perfectionist often torments herself with thoughts like *I'm lazy; I'm not doing anything.* When I have such a client, I sometimes walk into a session and greet her with, "What are you doing?" The response is usually, "Nothing!" After observing this little scenario for several sessions I often ask how it is that she can do nothing, for lying there dead is indeed "doing something." Watching television is indeed watching television. Sitting there resting is sitting there resting. Living by the principle of "I'd rather be accused of doing nothing than be accused of doing something wrong" is simply an effort to avoid criticism, which is seen as an attack on her self-esteem. In such a case, I ask the client to try to come in and report an activity in which she truly did nothing. Again, they find this quite difficult to do.

Perfectionism also may take the form of a troubled procrastinator who pounds herself with guilt. I remind her that to decide not to decide *is* also a decision. This often provokes some anxiety, as I have tampered with a major defense against criticism (her own as well as others), but out of the turmoil that is created growth can begin to take place.

The person with anorexia is often in this position in her refusal to gain weight, claiming she cannot. When reminded that putting off the decision for recovery is a decision, much anxiety usually results. That allows the counselor to evaluate the anxiety which is an obstacle to recovery.

After my pointing out the decision to put off recovery to one adolescent anorexic client, she fearfully stated, "If I get well, boys will want to date me, and I'm afraid of boys." We then explored her past traumatic experiences with boys and found them to consist of unpleasant teasing in the awkward years of junior high school. She also related sexual fears not uncommon at her age. As we desensitized her by our calm discussion of her problems, her fears abated and recovery progressed.

Throughout this phase of therapy, the healthy philosophy of the counselor is very important. With our gentle but firm support, with honest but noncondemning confrontations, the inborn curiosity of the little child in us all is again stimulated. The client's fears diminish and the process of personal growth is rekindled. We help them move away from the life described by Schopenhauer, "The purpose of life is to endure it," and toward a life that is an exciting adventure of discovery. Life can be full of interesting people to meet and experiences to share, for Jesus did come that we may "have life, and . . . have it more abundantly" (John 10:10 NKJV).

WORKS OR GRACE?

In many churches I have noticed a curious double-binding belief: you are damned if you do and damned if you don't; salvation is by grace and there's nothing we can do to earn it, yet you must be working like a slave or you're going to hell!

But just as one's spiritual salvation is not by works nor our goodness, but by forgiveness of one's badness, failures, and faults, so psychological healing is the result of accepting our weakness, failures, and faults. For as I accept them, I release great healing forces. "I have learned, in whatsoever state I am, therewith to be content" (Phil. 4:11 KJV). And "For every person will have to bear [be equal to understanding and calmly receive] his own (little) load [of oppressive faults]" (Gal. 6:5).

Teaching unconditional love is an emphasis that the pastoral counselor is specifically well prepared to make and it will contribute to the healing of persons with anorexia nervosa and bulimia.

CHAPTER TEN

THE WORST LITTLE GIRL IN THE WORLD
The Self-Esteem Factor

WE ALL KNOW HOW HARD IT IS to accomplish our goals. Think of how successful your last attempt was to keep a New Year's resolution. In a similar vein, a person with anorexia or bulimia is not only attempting to change her body image, but also in almost every area of her life she holds standards far beyond her reach. In fact, sometimes the only area in which she does feel somewhat successful is in the control of her weight by the compulsive rituals that emerge. This explains the sense of exhilaration the anorexic feels when she has lost another pound. That euphoria is in sharp contrast to the failure she feels in almost every other area of her life.

But there is a flip side to the success. People with eating

disorders realize that their eating behavior is somewhat socially deviant and, therefore, the victories in maintaining their weight or losing further weight are not accompanied with the social satisfaction that comes with their sharing. They can't share their joy and expect someone to rejoice with them. This ultimately leads them to the position of feeling unlovable, or as Thomas Harris would say "not okay." [1]

Any attempt to persuade a person with low self-esteem that she is better than she feels, that she is more loved than she perceives, only seems to reinforce that "not okay" position. Any attempt to build the client's self-respect and esteem only confirms to her that her perceptions and judgment are defective. Indeed, such people are able to rationalize this because they "know they are not okay"; if the counselor who thinks he or she is okay tells the patient that she is okay the patient is then apt to question the counselor's judgment, and see the counselor as "not okay" also. This major therapeutic impasse greatly frustrates the counselor unskilled in handling such illogical rationalizations.

Our Life Is the Tool to Break the Impasse

Again, it is important to mention the personality of the counselor. Unless I have learned to love myself as I am, with my strengths and weaknesses, with my successes and failures, with my altruism and sins, I will be unable to help the patient struggling with self-esteem problems. If the counselor believes that love of the patient is dependent upon the patient's performance or conformance to the counselor's expectations, if he or she looks down on the patient as inferior or misunderstands her struggle, the counselor will be as the blind leading the blind and success in therapy will be elusive. This deserves vital consideration because one of the first things the patient will do is test the counselor in this particular area, both behaviorally and verbally, checking out the therapist's own self-image.

For example, the anorexic patient will frequently give assent to the counselor's plans in the session and yet will not carry them out. Instead of denying or hiding her failure, she will consciously or unconsciously devise ways for the therapist to discover her lack of commitment. At the moment of discovery, the patient will be acutely aware of the counselor's response, including signs of frustration, disapproval or condemnation, the presence of which will essentially end the therapeutic relationship. Whatever else the counselor says after that will be suspect and ignored.

Some patients will actively challenge their counselors by pouncing on every apparent mistake with sarcasm, ridicule, and even overt anger. A skillful, nondefensive response will demonstrate the "okay" feeling you, the counselor, have about yourself. A defensive response or a counterattacking response will essentially end therapy as a process, although the patient may continue to come for sessions.

One day when a client angrily accused me of failing to make an appointment with her parents, I acknowledged that I indeed had forgotten and that I was concerned that she might interpret my forgetfulness as a lack of caring about the seriousness of her illness and about her problems. I observed that her anger immediately abated.

Treatment of Low Self-Esteem

The technical manner in which low self-esteem is addressed depends a great deal on the psychotherapeutic viewpoints and beliefs of the counselor. Many approaches have some benefit. Being eclectically trained, I find it useful to formulate several approaches from the various schools of theology, psychiatry, and psychology. This justifies my belief that although no one approach works for everyone, there is an approach that will work for each client, and strengthens my commitment not to give up my search for it until it has been identified. This engenders in myself an optimism for resolution that is important for the patient to observe and feel.

As we have stated, my basic approach to therapy is to focus on false beliefs and correct them. The most obvious first step in this is to help the patient become aware that she does not love herself or feel lovable. This often requires listening carefully to her choice of words, her response to praise or approval, and the tendency to denigrate herself frequently.

I remember listening to one girl's lengthy and repeated confessions of all the "bad" things she had done. Indeed, there was a long list of acting out behaviors that were quite destructive to herself, her health, and her relationship with her family and others. One day I remarked that she "must be the worst little girl in the world." She initially responded with hurt and anger; finally with frustration. When she looked at me, she saw my warm smile. I explained that I was only verbalizing what I was hearing and what it seemed she was feeling inside. Immediately, she recognized that this was true. She spent the next six sessions struggling with the enormity of that reality. In these sessions, I frequently greeted her with, "How is the worst little girl in the world doing?" Gradually as she became desensitized to the idea, her emotional reaction to the thought diminished and she finally came to believe, "I may be bad but I'm not that bad." When she arrived at that conclusion, her behavior began to improve as she no longer had to demonstrate to the world how badly she felt inside. In this case, this was the major turning point in her therapy.

Care Enough to Act

On occasion I have known bulimic patients who've become addicted to amphetamines and even to cocaine in their attempts to control their appetites. In a few of these instances, I have been able to obtain the names of the drug suppliers and have persuaded my clients that in pursuit of recovery it was essential that we cut off the sources and facilitate withdrawal from these substances. With some fears on both of our parts, we have provided names of the pushers to the narcotics division of the local police department and in each case the patient was eventually successful in her recovery. Although fear of retaliation from the pusher may have initially assisted in the patient's turning away from substance abuse, I believe the greatest reason for the recovery was her knowledge that I was willing to go to great lengths to fight against her illness and for her recovery. Again, the message is: You may have made some mistakes, but I am willing to care enough to go to great lengths to help you.

As We Forgive Ourselves We Are Able to Teach Others Forgiveness

Once the low self-esteem is recognized and acknowledged, I use my own personal character quirks as a tool in demonstrating my own acceptance of myself. This practice is especially useful if I can relate my own struggle to that of the client's. For example, with a bulimic who demonstrates significant impulsiveness, I relate incidences in which my own impulsiveness got me into trouble. With some humorous detail, I relate how I learned to cope with my problem, usually ending my anecdote saying that I'm about 80 percent cured.

With the compulsive anorexic, I tend to pick anecdotal experiences more related to my own struggles with perfectionism and the need to please others. I remind her that one has to be fairly compulsive to get into medical school and that I am a member in good standing of "Compulsives Anonymous." As I've stated previously it is compassionate encounters that really lead to the psychotherapeutic healing. Allowing myself to be a real person with real struggles that have real solutions helps facilitate the therapeutic process. I'm always on guard to ensure that the patient does not see this as bragging or stating that the process of change is quick or easy.

LOOK FOR CAUSES OF LOW SELF-WORTH

In my practice, an essential aspect of the therapy of low self-esteem also includes exploration of how the problem developed. The focus is not so much on the patient's own memory of past events, but rather on how that feeling of being unloved is currently being reinforced. When that is identified, we go to great lengths to change the situation if it is at all possible to do so.

For example, it is not at all uncommon for people with eating disorders to seek out relationships that are somewhat critical and punitive. Why? Because they want to find external controls for their uncontrollable actions. I always listen for signs of such situations where the patient works for a harsh, critical employer, dates a controlling, jealous boyfriend, or attends a legalistic, condemning church. Part of therapy may then be to consider a job change or to include the boyfriend in therapy sessions to teach him to become a therapeutic ally rather than be a part of the continuing problem. We may also have to address the religious distortion by ensuring that the patient clearly understands Christ's teaching about love and forgiveness. Often this is difficult for clients to deal with because they have been taught to not question their religious beliefs for fear their beliefs will somehow be destroyed or altered. Sometime in their past they may have been harshly condemned and/or punished for questioning the authority of another, whether it be parent, teacher, preacher, or doctor. I like to share with them a pearl of wisdom given to me in my college days by a very loving and wise minister: "Ray, there's a lot in the Bible that isn't in the church and there's a lot in the church that isn't in the Bible."

The thought was intriguing when I first heard it over thirty years ago, and with each passing day the profoundness of that statement has been clarified. That sentence has taught me to evaluate critically all the things I do and don't do, with the Bible as the ultimate authority against which I measure my beliefs and resulting behavior. That wise man's honest observation is a powerful tool in releasing my clients to reexamine their own beliefs in the light of the Bible. I especially direct their attention to the uncondemning love of God. At the same time, God, in his Word and in his works points out the consequences of our mistakes so that we can choose behaviors that will help us avoid the mistakes.

THE NEW BIRTH AS THE MODEL OF HEALING

The self-destructive behavior that is seen in many illnesses, including anorexia nervosa, bulimia, and obesity is often the direct result of the belief that sins must be punished, and ultimately by suffering and death. Proverbs 14:12 says, "There is a way that seems right to a man, but its end is the way of death" (NKJV). And I often wonder if one of those destructive beliefs is that sins *should* be punished rather than forgiven. This belief is the core of our harsh penal system, which seems to harden people's hearts rather than to lead them to a changed life. We see the harshness in an approach to child rearing that provokes angry, rebellious children; the condemnation that seems to strengthen a patient's illness and tenaciously grips her life rather than leading her to deliverance.

For those who have such religious distortions, I find Romans 3:23, 24, specifically useful: ". . . all have sinned and are falling short of the honor and glory which God bestows and receives.

[All] are justified and made upright and in right standing with God, freely and gratuitously by His grace (His unmerited favor and mercy), through the redemption which is [provided] in Christ Jesus." This makes sense of the bumper sticker that states, "Christians are not perfect, just forgiven," but, more than that, it gives the imperfect patient and me, the imperfect therapist, a point in common: We are both sinners saved by grace.

Paul went on to write in Romans 3:27: "Then what becomes of [our] pride and [our] boasting? It is excluded—banished, ruled out entirely. On what principle? [On the principle] of doing good deeds? No, but on the principle of faith." In contrast, then, the real plan of release from our guilt can be found in John 3:16 which every believer can quote from memory, "For God so loved the world, that he gave his only begotten Son, that whosoever believeth in him should not perish, but have everlasting life" (KJV). Presented more accurately in The Amplified Bible, it reads "For God so greatly loved and dearly prized the world that He [even] gave up His only-begotten (unique) Son, so that whoever believes in (trusts, clings to, relies on) Him shall not perish—come to destruction, be lost—but have eternal (everlasting) life." This says that identifying with Christ and incorporating his teachings into your very personality is essential for your new birth; merely believing that Christ is the Son of God is insufficient.

Some believe that confession of sin leads to the new birth, but confession alone is not enough. Many alcoholics, anorexics, and bulimics are finally willing to admit their illness, and although this is a step toward healing, does not result in life change. Confession must be coupled with repentance: "If My people who are called by My name shall humble themselves, pray, seek, crave and require of necessity My face, and turn from their wicked ways, then will I hear from Heaven, forgive their sin, and heal their land" (2 Chron. 7:14). This plan of salvation requires confession, not like a criminal pleading for mercy, but the simple, confident acknowledgment of sins and repentance, which in the Hebrew means "to turn about and go in another direction" or "turn from our wicked ways"; it does not imply remorse, penitence, weeping, wailing, gnashing of teeth, self-flagellation, or self-blame. When we do confess,

God will come and forgive our sins and heal our land. In the New Testament, repentance is associated with being transformed by the renewing of one's mind (Rom. 12:2). This is the theological basis of cognitive therapy in which distorted or irrational beliefs (even theological beliefs) are replaced with the truth. The results of the transformed beliefs can then be seen in changes in our feelings and actions.

Self-condemning confessions fly in the face of Christ's continuation of John 3:16—"For God did not send the Son into the world in order to judge—to reject, to condemn, to pass sentence on—the world; but that the world might find salvation and be made safe and sound through Him" (v. 17). This requires that the client learn to cease condemning herself and that she replace condemnation with caring for herself as God cares for her. The practice of this concept teaches the patient that unconditional love exists and that the solution to error is not in condemnation or punishment, but in forgiveness and mercy.

It is my belief that the sacrament of communion is indeed illustrative of the salvation process. Just as the bread and the wine are literally incorporated into our flesh and blood, so we must incorporate Christ's Spirit through his Word and his works into our very personality. This is a process which Christ does with us rather than to us or for us.

Other Areas to Explore

After going through the steps and dealing with the issues outlined to this point, I usually see the visible effects of a patient's new optimism, and a brightening of mood. If I do not see a glimpse of this after four to six months of therapy, I often look to other approaches to deal with the self-esteem problem. Examples are the use of the concrete diagrams of Transactional Analysis which often identify a "punitive parent" component to the client's mind that speaks with excessive harshness to the "bad child." [2] Evidence of this may surface in conversation about the past and/or the present.

This brings to mind my work with a young secretary who early in therapy made repeated statements like "I am dumb, stupid, or crazy." With such self-critical statements coming from her "punitive parent" she felt like a "bad child." After a period of time, I began to bring these statements to her attention. I suggested that she modify her expressions at least by saying, "although I am generally intelligent, I at times do 'dumb' things." With continued reinforcement, she began to change her thoughts about herself. As surely as water flows downhill, her feelings began to change also.

Sometimes a traumatic event has triggered the eating disorder and you may have to dig deeper to find out what it was. This could be a breakup with a boyfriend to whom the young woman was unduly attached. If this is the case, it is important to help the broken-hearted young woman grieve the loss, both of the relationship and of the self-esteem that can feel so permanently damaged after such a crisis. Indeed, only after she goes through the phases of disbelief, anger, search for cause, and the experience of pain can she get on with the rebuilding of her life and resolve the "John doesn't love me, therefore no man can love me" distortion, which is an overgeneralization.

Another common scenario was the coach who was reinforcing the cognitive distortion that if the long-distance runner could get her body fat content down to below 10 percent of body weight, she would be able to win an Olympic medal. Winning became the only goal, and losing was unacceptable. I picked up my dictaphone and started a letter.

For several years, I have written many letters to university presidents, headmasters, principals, coaches and sports-medicine physicians in our school systems in the attempt to immobilize such unhealthy practices. All of these efforts on my part demonstrate to the client that I indeed do care about and for her and that my love is not merely "in theory or in speech but in deed and in truth—in practice and in sincerity" (1 John 3:18).

On occasion I find patients who seem disinterested in understanding their low self-esteem. I am indebted to Dr. Sig Weedman, my close associate of fifteen years for sharing with me the following story which we have both found useful in working with such clients.

A Useful Parable About Susie

When Susie was a little girl, her parents were struggling financially and yet were quite concerned about looking good to the surrounding world. One day they went out to buy a full-length mirror to hang behind the door so that every morning before they went out into the world, they could check to make sure they looked presentable. Because they didn't have much money, they shopped around to find a good buy. They found a mirror that had a flaw near the bottom that gave a distorted image, but because they were tall, the flaw wouldn't bother them. They bought it anyway.

Unfortunately, one day, as little Susie was toddling around the house, she came into the room and saw herself in the mirror. She said, "My, I look funny. I don't look like my playmates so I must be a funny-looking kid." Everyday after play she'd go back and look into the mirror and she'd say, "I don't look like Jane. I don't look like Mary. I am a funny-looking kid." Because of this, she became increasingly careful about the kind of friends she had. Susie didn't want to expose herself to kids who would tell her she was funny looking. She believed if she played with them too much, they might notice that she was different. And so she had few friends during her early childhood. Interestingly, those friends she did have didn't seem to notice her unusual appearance.

The day came when Susie grew old enough to go to school. Regarding this she thought, *As long as I'm at home I'm safe where kids can't call me names and tell me I'm funny looking, so I'm not going to school.* But then she had an idea. *At Halloween when kids come by, they all have masks on. Then you cannot really see what they look like. Maybe if I can have a mask to wear I can go to school.* So Susie went into the kitchen, found a paper sack and scissors, and proceeded to make herself a mask. With this mask, Susie was able to go to school. She knew that people couldn't see what she looked like if she had a sack over her head. Susie felt safe behind the mask and thought, *Nobody will know I'm a funny-looking kid.* Of course, the people in school thought it was unusual that a child would be there with a paper sack over her head and they kept their distance, wondering if she had some horrible illness that she was attempting to hide from the world.

As the years passed, Susie often wondered why kids wouldn't ask her to come to their houses to play, to eat lunch with them, or to play in their games. But each day, upon arrival home, she would run to the mirror, take off her paper sack, and peer intently. Sure enough, she was still a funny-looking kid and she became more and more grateful for the sack. Susie thought perhaps if she changed sacks she could appeal to the children differently. So she tried a Safeway sack, and a Sears sack, and a Penney's sack, but somehow it didn't matter—the kids still treated her with distance. Susie continued to grow up convinced that somehow others knew that under the paper sack was a funny-looking kid.

Years passed and Susie went away to college. By this time, she had looked into her mirror thousands of times and each time was convinced that if kids ever saw her face, she would have no friends, because she did indeed look different from the others.

If we interrupt the story for a moment and think about this story, we find that each of us, from childhood on up, has seen ourselves in mirror relationships. Because these relationships reflect back a perception of ourselves as others see us, we can see how we develop distorted views of ourselves. Therefore, just as Susie looked at herself in a damaged mirror and got a distorted view of herself, so we have received distorted views of ourselves as people have labeled us as ugly, dumb, bad, unlovable, lazy, stupid, fat, skinny, or weak.

When Susie finally finished her education, she decided to enter the job market and begin an independent life. She was able to find a tolerant employer who said that, even though she wore a paper sack, she could come and work for him. So she did. Again she noticed that her fellow employees looked at her kind of funny; they didn't stop and talk to her at the water cooler, nor did they invite her to eat lunch with them.

Finally, one of the other employees looked at Susie and thought, *I've never seen anything like this before. I wonder what happened to this woman to make her always wear a paper sack over her head?* So she gathered up her courage, met Susie at the water cooler, and said, "Would you like to have lunch with me?"

This startled Susie a bit and she thought, *What's your angle? What do you want from me?* She gave a noncommital, "Yes, that would be nice sometime."

The fellow employee persisted until Susie finally acquiesced and said she'd join her on Tuesday. This gracious person seemed oblivious to the mask, friendly, and interested.

Susie, with her skepticism, wondered, *Why do you want to talk to someone who underneath all of this is obviously a funny-looking kid?* With the persistence of her friend, the two women started having lunch together frequently. After months went by, they stopped at the water cooler one day and the friend asked if Susie would come to her home for dinner. By this time Susie's trust had grown. If the friend was willing to risk having lunch with such a funny-looking kid, maybe an evening meal together would be all right as well. In time, Susie's confidence and security grew when she was with the friend and, of course, the friend noticed.

One day she said, "Susie, I just have to ask you something. I've noticed that you always wear a paper sack over your head. But, now that I've gotten to know you, I find that you are kind, although timid, and easy to be a friend to. I really wonder why you must wear this paper sack."

Susie decided she would risk telling her friend the story of her life. She shared how as a young child she had looked in a mirror and found that she did not look like other kids and that the solution to her embarrassment was to hide in a paper sack. She told how she had done that for years, never risking taking off the paper sack because she didn't want anyone to know that she was a funny-looking kid.

Her friend thought for a while and said, "I've been willing to be your friend when you've worn a paper sack over your head. Would you be willing to let me know you as you are?" Then she asked if the mirror was still in existence.

Susie said yes, her family still lived in the town. Although she didn't live with them anymore, they still had the same mirror.

The friend wanted to see it, and so she and Susie arranged to examine the mirror. Before they went, the friend went out and bought five good mirrors that accurately reflected the images before them. The two women met at Susie's family's home and went to look at the mirror. At a glance the friend saw what the problem was. She thought to herself, *That mirror is distorted, as I suspected. I wonder if Susie would be willing to take her mask off and look at these five mirrors and then look at the distorted mirror to see if she would notice a difference?*

At this suggestion, Susie said, "I haven't had this mask off in the presence of another human being for years. But you have been a friend to me when no one else has, so I will try it."

She slipped the sack off and looked in the old mirror only to find she still looked the same as always. Then she looked into the new mirrors and thought, *I do look different in these mirrors.*

The friend asked, "How does it feel to see yourself in the old mirror?"

Susie said, "Well, I feel kind of sad and odd; I don't feel like I'm part of the human race. I feel like an outsider. But it is familiar and I feel comfortable looking at the image because I'm used to it. The images in the new mirrors don't look like me—they look like somebody else. In fact, I feel kind of anxious when I look into the new mirrors, but they do give me hope that perhaps I can become like other people."

Susie's friend said, "Perhaps we need another opinion. I'd like you to gather your courage to come to work someday without your paper sack. Let's see what happens."

What a frightening thought—to go out into the world unprotected by those defenses that she had been used to all of those years. But with the knowledge that her friend would be there, she thought she could try it.

When that special day arrived, she had to concentrate on the decision because it had become such a habit each morning to reach for her sack before going out the door. That day she left the sack on the shelf and went to work. The people who were used to her sack noticed a little bit but didn't react excessively and so Susie decided to try it another day. Her habit was so ingrained that some days she would get to work and then notice she had unconsciously put the sack back on her head. Susie realized that habits of two decades don't vanish overnight. She did notice that people came up to her at the water cooler more than they had before. A few other people invited her out to lunch. And gradually—gradually—over a period of time, the feeling that she was a "funny-looking kid" began to diminish. She felt more a part of the human race and felt less different from other people. With the help of her friends, she ultimately resolved her false image—that she thought she was a funny-looking kid.

This story demonstrates how self-esteem problems may arise from seeing oneself in the mirror of distorted relationships. It suggests that resolution requires someone caring enough to notice the struggle, to notice the paper sack and offer the love, acceptance, and encouragement needed to risk removing the defenses so that the person can begin to see herself as she really is. We all need somebody who loves us enough to tell us the truth.

A ROLE FOR THE FAMILY IN SELF-ESTEEM REPAIR

When working with the parents or spouses of eating disorder patients, I generally ask that they be responsible for helping me improve the self-esteem of their daughters or wives. To clarify a family's responsibility, I clearly state that the eating practices and weight control of the patient will be the domain of the patient and myself. The family is usually relieved to hear that this area is not theirs to worry about. I also inform them that they should talk with me when any concerns about weight or eating practices arise. If they do not, their own anxieties will rise to the point that family communication will disintegrate and the eating practices may once again become the focus of a power struggle.

In attending to the self-esteem, I ask parents or spouses to take the role of participant observers. In doing so, I am asking them to improve their accuracy as mirrors in which patients see themselves. I suggest that they begin to make lists of the patients' strengths and weaknesses, encouraging them to point out two strengths for every weakness. If strong feelings have been running rampant, I encourage them at first to present these observations to the patient in the form of letters. Often the families struggle a great deal with this. They have been so focused on the negative and see so little of the positive that they often need help from the counselor in this regard. With some prodding, it is generally easy for parents to point out their daughter's intelligence, good recall, action-oriented nature, or strong will. It is equally easy to point out her impulsiveness and her lack of good judgment, which, although appropriate for her age, are obviously inadequate to cope with her eating disorder. The following letter was shared with me by a family who followed up on this suggestion with great skill.

Dear Christy,

So you won't misunderstand how I see you and feel about you, I'd like to write to you and attempt to put on paper my thoughts and feelings. I hope you will think about what I say and talk with me about any points that are unclear or with which you disagree.

I want to state very clearly to you that I *care* very much for you; I will never stop being concerned about you, your growth, and development; I will do my best to protect you from others as well as from yourself. No matter what happens in the future, I will never give up on you, so you are stuck with me as your father. Your mother and I are your strongest allies and have repeatedly demonstrated this in confronting problems with teachers, counselors, neighbors, and your friends.

First, I would like to point out a few areas in your life and personality which need improvement. As I stated recently, your judgment (ability to make wise decisions) is only that of a fourteen-year-old, but that is how old you are. A major error is that you feel that you are more capable than you really are. Of course that feeling usually occurs in people your age. An example of this is that you are more concerned about what you put on your hair than you are about your choice of words, or the food you eat. You are also more concerned about what you wear than about your attitudes toward yourself and others. Not that external appearance is unimportant, but that personality is equally important. I do realize it is easier to work on our outward appearance than it is to work on our personality. Still, it is our personality that lasts while styles continually change. Our habits, attitudes, and choice of words stay.

You are well aware of your impulsiveness which is both a strength and a weakness. It helps you be an action person, a real doer like me; yet there is a tendency for both of us to act first and think about it later. That can keep us in trouble until our judgment improves.

As important is your ability to do what is right in spite of pressure from friends to do otherwise; you can be a true leader and show your friends a better way. With your strong personality, your friends do look up to you as an example. You all can benefit when you use your leadership to help them improve their study habits during the school year, and to improve the way they handle conflicts with their friends and families.

Two of your greatest strengths are that you learn quickly and you forgive the mistakes of others quickly. That should help very much as we resolve the conflicts between us. Also, although you still experience periods of moodiness when you are feeling irritable, they seem to pass more quickly (especially with rest) and then you are cooperative, hard working, charming, alive, and fun. I have seen great improvement in your moods in the past year, especially when working with me on your schoolwork. I am really pleased with this. I hope we can use this summer to improve our ability to work out conflicts. I know being fourteen is not easy. Bear with us and the future will be bright, filled with joy not mere excitement.

> Love,
> Dad

The change in attitude of the parents from being critical and controlling to caringly confrontive, as represented in this letter, was the turning point in Christy's recovery.

This area of low self-esteem is where the pastoral counselor can make the greatest contribution. He or she can bring the messages of the unconditional love of God and forgiveness of sin which are lacking in secular therapy and the usual medical practice. Secular therapy usually deals with guilt by stating that sin is not sin and this can lead to more chaos.[3] It is my opinion that a spiritual experience of new birth, when accomplished with awareness, is the only truly effective antidote for the poison of guilt.

CHAPTER ELEVEN

WHAT IS A WOMAN?
The Sexual Identity Factor

HEADLINES LIKE "Women want work as well as marriage!" make it clear that women are being pressured to adopt a wide variety of roles: employee, boss, mother, wife, girlfriend, professional. With women being pulled from every side, is it any wonder that many feel confused about what they would like to be when they grow up? In years past when life was simpler, femininity was defined in functional terms, and the growing girl learned the skills necessary to wait on her family with much denial of her own wants and needs. That simple definition has been increasingly challenged and *is* undoubtedly oversimplified. Indeed, we can see that Christ addressed this issue when he said, "Martha, Martha, you are anxious and troubled about many things; There is need of (but a few things, or) only one.

Mary has chosen the good portion . . . which shall not be taken away from her" (Luke 10:41,42). I suspect that there has always been some confusion regarding the appropriate social role for a woman.

When the "Who am I?" question is raised, it is easy to simplify answers by thinking and talking in terms of appearance. Perhaps this is why you see some churches' preoccupation with questions such as, should women wear makeup, should they cut their hair, should they wear blue jeans or is that an unwomanly practice. To end the confusion, society often looks to an authority to give grand and wise answers and so the fashion industry has grown. Unfortunately, the leaders have shown poor judgment as they have selected poor role models even in the area of appearance. It is as though we have allowed a few "artists," who became preoccupied with the appearance of sickly, possibly tubercular, women of Paris, to set the standards by which beauty is now judged. In the attempt to maintain the emaciated appearances anorexia nervosa is now an occupational hazard of professional models, and I have seen several in my practice.

As I previously noted, rather well-designed surveys have indicated that 85 percent of American women feel that they are too fat, while only about 15 percent of the American population is obese according to current definitions of obesity (see chapter 7). Even though this 15 percent may underrepresent women and overrepresent men, perceived reality is a world away from true reality.

If we look at historic art, such as the statue *Venus de Milo*, probably made in the first or second century B.C., or the *Birth of Venus*, a painting by Botticelli (1478 A.D.), we see that earlier generations had a standard of physical beauty for women undoubtedly closer to the data presented by the Metropolitan Life Insurance tables.

WHEN LOOKING GOOD IS NOT GOOD

This shows that there is a major false belief in our culture— that truth is established through consensus rather than by data. Therefore, the idea that "Thin is beautiful" is one of eating disorders' false premises most difficult to combat. The individual must learn to stand against social pressures for conformity and, instead, base her decisions upon scientific reality.

Yet this is easier said than done. When we observe nations "liquidating deviationists" such as in Ethiopia and Afghanistan; when we hear of the treatment of Christians in Russia, or Jews in Iran, we know that it does take an unusual degree of courage to stand on principle. If one's stance is too different from societal norms, he or she is like a leper—thrust outside the camp. With this background in mind, do not be too harsh on the young woman who anxiously looks at *Teen* magazine or *Vogue* as she attempts to select her dress for the day; don't be too harsh when you observe teenagers anxiously looking into the mirror for the sign of a pimple or a bulging waistline. As William Glasser said in *Schools Without Failure,* the basic problem of every student is not academics but "saving face." [1]

Think of what registers in our children's minds when they hear of the high pay of the very slender models selected by anxious managers of leading department stores—managers who look to the same fashion magazines that the adolescents do. Indeed, one of my very attractive young patients became bulimic when she was turned down for a modeling job with the statement, "Don't come back until you can show me bones." Is it any wonder that bulimia followed?

How about the long-distance runner whose anorexia began when her coach stated that a body-fat content of less than 10 percent would be necessary if she were to be really successful? (Scientific study shows us that a woman's body goes into hormonal chaos if body fat drops below about 18 percent.) Or how about the advertisement on national television, "You can't be too rich or too thin"? Fortunately, the various anorexia and bulimia associations of America were sufficiently well-organized to solicit a flood of adverse mail and that ad was withdrawn.

Pressure to Conform

Our churches, schools, and courts of law place a heavy emphasis on submission to authority. Is it any wonder that our adolescent children, searching for their identities, anxiously seek out authorities for criteria by which they can determine whether or not they are indeed "okay." Go to any junior high or high school and you will be struck by the uniformity of appearance. Before condemning them for being a weak-willed bunch of sheep, notice how anxiously our politicians consult the latest polls before deciding how they will vote. For them too, taking the popular course of action is more important than selecting the appropriate course of action. It is more important to give bread and circuses to the people than to be financially prudent. Or notice how parents guide their children by asking, "What will the neighbors think?" rather than "What is best for you?"

When I first started working with eating disorders, the oral impregnation theory was popular among therapists in this field. The essence of this theory was that when a little girl observed a pregnant woman, the girl thought the pregnant woman was getting fat; therefore, she concluded, eating too much made one pregnant. The anorexic girl stopped eating for fear of getting pregnant.[2] I was continually impressed with how difficult it was for me to convince fellow therapists that eating disorders were primarily mood and identity problems. Though I continually confirmed my observations by studying the lives of people who came to me, the literature seemed to be eternally espousing theories quite foreign to my experiences. It was indeed comforting when data-base scientists, such as Harrison Pope,[3] James Hudson,[4] and Craig Johnson,[5] presented data that helped me feel more confident in my own observations. Again, this demonstrates the importance of determining reality by appealing to data rather than authority. Historically, authorities have frequently been incorrect.

Perhaps this is why the strong men and women of the Bible said they had to serve God and not man. It reinforces the truth of that song sung in children's church, "Dare to be a Daniel, dare to stand alone." Perhaps we as parents, as counselors, as religious leaders need to encourage our children to think a bit more independently, even if it leads to what seems like conflict and rebellion. Perhaps we should have them pay more attention to the logic of the situation and not allow the solution to the conflict to be based merely on a battle of wills. This requires, however, that we develop the first skill of the scientist: to be a good witness and set aside the arrogance of the judge who thinks he knows right from wrong, truth from falsehood. Indeed, we must remember the one who told Adam and Eve that if they ate of the fruit of the garden they would become like gods, knowing right from wrong. The one who said that was the great Deceiver.

What Is Healthy?

Fortunately, the powerful fitness movement assists us in helping the young woman with an eating disorder clarify her identity relative to her bodily appearance. Unfortunately, roots of the cognitive distortion of thinness still need to be eliminated as we replace the word *thin* with the word *trim*. What is needed is a model of feminine appearance selected scientifically by comparative studies determining optimum levels of function, coupled with the morbidity and mortality studies such as those done by the Metropolitan Life Insurance Company. At this point, such studies are fragmented but, as time progresses, I would hope the emerging knowledge will become integrated into a complete picture of what a woman's ideal weight should be.

Good health rests on four legs: appropriate diet, appropriate exercise, necessary rest, and a positive mental attitude. In each of these areas it is important to determine just what is appropriate for each individual.

Appropriate Food Is Important

It is increasingly obvious that our diets are indeed healthier if we consume more vegetables, whole grains, and fruits while reducing the consumption of simple sugars and carbohydrates, namely white sugar and white flour.[6] Athletes may also require diets higher in complex carbohydrates than nonathletes.[7] Also contributing to improved health is the reduction of fats, especially saturated fats found in red meat, butter, and coconut oil. Yet simply replacing saturated fats with unsaturated doesn't seem to be the answer. By significantly increasing the unsaturated fats in the diet, the risk of heart disease goes down but the risk of cancer goes up. Current consensus calls for about a 50–50 balance between saturated and unsaturated fats. It may well be that using butter on our bread and safflower oil in our salad dressing is a good dietary practice. Americans are eating less red meat than they have in the past, and the probable increase in the consumption of poultry and fish will no doubt provide evidence that something in fish oils reduces both cholesterol and triglycerides in the blood, with the cardiovascular protection that seems to result.

Scientists are also recognizing that a reduction of salt is beneficial, although some studies have shown that as sodium chloride is reduced, other salts should be increased.[8] Indeed, where a little selenium is present in the drinking water, rates of hypertension are reduced; where calcium is present in the drinking water, heart disease is reduced;[9] where a little fluoride is in the drinking water, teeth are strengthened, and heart attacks reduced;[10] where lithium is present in the drinking water, moods are stabilized and acts of violence diminish.[11]

The reader may be wondering why we have discussed nutrition in a section on female identity, and I would remind you that folklore tells us, "You are what you eat." Although it is much more complicated than that, a visit to the vitamin section in a pharmacy will reveal vitamin and mineral preparations made specifically for women. Such preparations recognize that women's bodies need different amounts of some minerals, such as calcium and iron, than do men's bodies. Pregnant and lactating women have different needs still, and specific vitamin and mineral preparations are prepared for them also.

Unfortunately, there are large gaps in our knowledge about specific nutritional differences between women and men. We know that women generally are protected against coronary artery disease until menopause. Does this mean that their bodies require higher amounts of fats in their diets? We have suggested earlier in chapter 5 that the excessive craving for food experienced by patients may be partially caused by unknown nutritional deficiencies. Certainly the body of the anorexic patient needs nutritional supplements, including a vitamin and mineral preparation designed for a woman's body. Isn't it curious that the nursery rhyme of our childhood acknowledges the difference? But it must be not as simple as "sugar and spice and everything nice, that's what little girls are made of" versus "snips and snails and puppy dogs' tails, that's what little boys are made of."

Exercise Balanced with Rest Is Important

The studies indicating that exercise improves our moods through the stimulation of an internal, natural, morphinelike substance (beta endorphin) complement what we are learning about healthy eating.[12] We see that even exercise can be carried to absurd limits and become unhealthy when not balanced with times of restorative rest. This is often seen in the frantic exercise of the anorexic attempting to maintain a weight below what is healthy. Rest repairs the body structurally, releasing a growth hormone that stimulates protein synthesis, and also allows the excessive breakdown products of busy metabolism to be eliminated and a neurohormonal transmitter substance to be restored so that we can think clearly and enjoy life.

Although data is still fragmented and far from complete, this amount of available information is sufficient to persuade the population that we must continue to walk away from the cognitive distortion that "you can't be too rich or too thin" and toward the healthy quest for trimness as generally found in the physical fitness movement.

WHAT IS A WOMAN?

On the other hand, I am very much concerned that we emphasize too much the physical side of femininity and not enough the emotional and cognitive needs. Unfortunately, it is easier to deal with the numbers on a scale than with the matters of the heart and this is why, in my opinion, weight is often singled out as the problem. In guiding people to recovery, weight is the least important issue. I spend much less time talking about diet, calories, and the scale than the question, "Who are you?"

I believe that the quest for thinness comes out of the desire to be loved. The sick individual believes that she is unloved and therefore unlovable. Some of this may be traced back to our previous discussions of perfectionism and low self-esteem, and the dissonance between them. More specifically, I find this is especially important in the area of sexual identity.

Eric Berne implied that the sparkle in the eye of a girl comes from the approval of her father.[13] I suppose the corollary may also be true, that the confidence in a son comes from the approval of his mother. In either case, the parent of the opposite sex has a very important role in validating the sexuality of the child.

Eric Berne went on to say that the parent of the opposite sex tells us what to do and the parent of the same sex shows us how to do it. The father says or implies, "Be pretty like your mother," and the little girl looks to her mother as the model of "prettiness." If he says, "Be competent like your mother," the little girl looks to mother for her skills.

Unfortunately, if one or both of the parents is dysfunctional, the modeling will be unhealthy and inappropriate. The child will not identify with the inappropriate parent and, without identification, will not incorporate the attitudes, beliefs, and practices of that parent. For example, if the mother is too controlling, too depressed, too passive, or too sick, the daughter may attempt to rebel against that model and try to become the opposite. However, as Eric Berne points out, the child risks developing a counterscript that is often just as unhealthy as the script itself. For example, if the mother is too fat, the daughter may become too thin. If the mother is too passive, the daughter may become overly active. If the mother is too controlling, the daughter may become too submissive. More often, I find that, without alternative models presented, the controlling mother produces a controlling daughter, the eating disorder being the area in which the daughter attempts to be controlling, not only of her own body but, through the threat implied by the illness, of the entire family.

If the marriage relationship is dysfunctional and/or the father-daughter relationship impaired, it will be difficult for the daughter to develop healthy relationships with men. First, her own identity as a woman may be insecure and she will relate from a position of uncertainty and insecurity. Out of such insecurity, she may feel such fear of a relationship that men will be avoided. If she does approach a relationship, it will be with ambivalence. Many mixed messages will lead to confusion for both the woman and the man. For example, many bulimic women I have treated seek out men to date whom they would never marry. This allows them to feel attractive yet avoids the revelations of inadequacy that a committed, intimate relationship would uncover.

With an insecure identity, a woman will be unduly vulnerable to hurt, if a romantic relationship ends. She will be flooded with self-doubts, grief, and despair. As she searches for the cause of her pain, a common concern is that her beauty was not sufficient to hold the relationship together. It is easy to see how this is an optimum condition for the development of an eating disorder.

As you can see, the role of the counselor is to carefully evaluate each situation to discern which factors are operational, then to design a plan to turn the family toward appropriate models of behavior. When the family dynamics contribute significantly to the illness, the family must become involved in the recovery process, if it is to be rapid and complete.

Sometimes, if the father and mother's relationship is strained, the father may encourage his daughter to become "Daddy's little girl." In this situation, anorexia and bulimia can surface because of a father's unconscious wish that his daughter never grow up and become capable of leaving the family. I have had several patients with eating disorders who, after a parental divorce, became comforters of their fathers who rewarded them in turn by paying all of their expenses, destroying their initiative, and thus creating helpless, dependent daughters who could not leave home.

I've also treated young women who have had one parent die. The eating disorder allowed a continuing symbiotic relationship between the surviving parent and the daughter; the grieving parent is comforted by the grieving daughter and the thought of the daughter growing away from the parent is too terrible for either party to contemplate.

Sometimes the trouble begins in adolescence when fathers are threatened by the thought that their daughters are becoming beautiful women. This awareness of their daughters' sexuality may provoke so much guilt, that the father and daughter spend the rest of their relationship fighting, which in turn ensures that considerable distance is kept between them.

Counselors must give fathers permission to express their love, appreciation, and approval of their daughters and teach them to do so by their own example. We need to help them know that one can operate within healthy limits that are essential to the emergence of a daughter's healthy identity.

If the mother is depressed and preoccupied with obsessions of perfectionism, we need to provide for her the appropriate treatment to bring her relief as well as relief to her troubled daughter. By so doing we are attempting to bring health to the whole family, when they are available to participate in the therapeutic process.

The greatest obstacle I find to family involvement in the therapeutic process is parental guilt. Parents feel that they have somehow caused their child's illness. The most common question I hear in the first parental session is, "What did we do wrong, Doctor?"

This allows me to point out the difference between searching for blame and understanding the process of the illness. This initial response of parents leads me to believe that guilt is one of the major obstacles to human personality change. If in therapy we must examine thoughts, feelings, and behavior, how can we proceed if the pain of guilt is too intense to bear? It is only possible for someone to go through the process of personal evaluation if he or she has access to forgiveness for error in the context of an unconditionally loving relationship.

WOMEN ARE PEOPLE TOO

Finally, when talking about a healthy concept of womanhood, I suggest to my clients that a woman can be a healthy partner of a man. I've come to believe in collaborative marriage, "a process in which two lives that are different are blended into a working unit in which the potential of each is developed to its highest level." [14]

I presented concepts of this type of relationship to Dan and Cherry O'Neill. Being bright, action-oriented people, the O'Neills immediately tried living by these concepts and, with equal rapidity, found Cherry's health restored. Dan became enthused about the principles presented and strongly encouraged me to write about them; as a result our book, *Marrying for Life*, emerged. The book contains the simple observation that when people of good will work together in harmony, they can put people on the moon. If this works to put people on the moon, people can certainly use these principles to work out problems in relationships, avoid divorce, improve health, find financial security and peace of mind, and, ultimately reach any goal that is useful to them.

To help a woman clarify an identity, it is essential for the counselor to have skill in validating others. This requires the ability to help people discover their skills and interests so they can build lives upon strengths rather than weaknesses. The counselor must also encourage the client to love herself with her weakness. In this process a woman counselor can be particularly effective, if she has worked through her own identity and is comfortable in it.

After all, a woman is a real human being, deserving of and capable of obtaining respect and love. She can become a partner with her counselor as they work responsibly together to regain her health. From that experience, she can learn more skillfully to collaborate with her father, an employer, a husband, and, ultimately, with her God.

CHAPTER TWELVE

TO BE OR NOT TO BE?
The Depression Factor

ONE DAY, SIXTEEN YEARS AGO, I was sitting in my office talking
with an emaciated sixteen-year-old girl who was telling me how
fat she felt. She lived with an alcoholic father and a mother
who had recurring breakdowns. In these conditions, she felt
that life just wasn't worth living. During our conversation the
thought came to me that if she were seventy years old and
revealed a somatic delusion coupled with a rapid weight loss
and a helpless, hopeless attitude, I would diagnose a psychotic
depression rather than an eating disorder. I would rush her
off to the hospital for vigorous, life-saving treatment. At that
moment I began to treat the depressive aspect of her illness
and, to my surprise, she began to improve.

As other emaciated women came to me for treatment, I always looked for signs of depression. Such evidence was usually visible and often there was a family history of depression.

When Cherry O'Neill came to me for help with her eating disorder (in 1977), I quickly saw elements of a mood disturbance. We began to explore how her beliefs affected her moods. Within a month she was started on an antidepressant, mood-stabilizing medication and her response was rapid. She completed the intensive phase of her treatment after only six months but continued occasional therapeutic contacts during the ensuing two years.

As people read her gripping book, *Starving for Attention,* they often identify strongly with her struggles against her illness, and especially with her struggle against depression. Her book is an excellent description of treatment, which included a combination of cognitive-behavioral changes coupled with antidepressant medication judiciously selected. [1]

In her more recent book, *Dear Cherry,* she describes a relapse in her mood disorder, due to a postpartum depression after the premature birth of her second child. [2] This was quickly identified and treatment with antidepressant medication brought a rapid and dramatic response. This indicates that she must be aware of a physiologic tendency toward depression that may require treatment on occasion, especially during times of biologic stress.

In my opinion her rapid response to treatment, both the first time for anorexia and the second time for depression, was due to accurate diagnosis and to the rapid administration of a comprehensive treatment plan. In addition, Cherry was in an opportune situation, having a supportive family, especially a husband who encouraged the cognitive changes necessary for her recovery. Cherry's own attitude was one of openness to change, having indeed suffered enough.

WHAT JOB'S STORY TEACHES ABOUT DEPRESSION

When dealing with the depressive aspects of an eating disorder, it is absolutely essential that the counselor avoid becoming a "Job's comforter." If you recall the story of Job, you'll remember that it is a description of a man whose life was pleasing to

God, but who became very depressed after many losses. His emotional pain is vividly described in Job 1:20–21; 2:12–13; and 3:1–26. If his symptoms are compared with descriptions of depression in more recent authoritative books such as Nathan Kline's, *From Sad to Glad*,[3] the similarity is inescapable. Job's story indicates that depression can come into anyone's life, the good, the bad, the rich, the poor, the just, and the unjust— none are immune.

Job's is indeed a classic story in that it describes depression with all of its features. Not only do we see his despair (to the point of wishing he had not been born), but also his boils, which signify that infection may accompany depression. Today, three millennia later, science has determined that, in depression, the immune system is impaired. Studies of the immune function in grieving people have shown that certain white blood cells (T-lymphocytes) are immobilized. If working properly, T-lymphocytes stimulate other white blood cells (beta-lymphocytes) to produce antibodies that are essential for our war against bacteria and viruses.[4] We now know why it is not unusual for death to claim a grieving widow or widower. A grieving person whose immune system is impaired may come down with a cold that rapidly progresses to pneumonia that is unresponsive to modern medical treatment. Job's boils were just a less severe form of this phenomenon.

Remember Job's wife, who asked him to curse God and die? I suggest that we be somewhat gentle and compassionate toward her, as she was a grieving mother. She had lost all of her children, and her words came out of a grieving heart.

One of the major messages in the story of Job is that we should avoid acting like Job's comforters, who were well-meaning but incompetent (through ignorance) to help someone in trouble. The error Job's friends made was in assuming they knew the cause of his problems. They accused him of hidden sins in his life after God had already stated that Job's sickness was not the result of Job's sin. God had said that Job was like no one else, "a blameless and upright man" (Job 1:8). Oh! If God were saying that about us!

The depressed anorexic client is also frequently accused of being at fault for her illness. But is it really her fault that society sees thinness as beauty? Is it really her fault that she, at an early age, heard the taunts of unwise children directed at someone a bit overweight, "Fatty, fatty, two-by-four, can't get through the kitchen door"? Is it really her fault that her family was not supportive when a boyfriend said, "Let's just be friends," causing her heart to break? Is it really her fault that she grieved alone because there was no one to mourn with her when her mother died? Is it really her fault that her parents endowed her with a genetic heritage that included vulnerability to depression? With so many false accusations, is it not clear why her misery is compounded and life isn't worth living?

With Job's own personal torment, compounded by the jabs from his friends, is it any wonder that Job regretted the day of his birth? That he even considered suicide? He said, "Why should I take my flesh in my teeth, and *put my life in my hand* [incurring the danger of God's wrath]? [I do it because though He slay me, yet will I wait for and trust Him . . .]" (Job 13:14, 15). Is such trust the answer to suicide for the Christian?

Job's Counselor

If we examine the story more closely, we find that a young man named Elihu stepped forth and said:

I am young, and you are aged; for that reason I was timid and restrained, and dared not declare my opinion to you. I said, Age should speak, and a multitude of years should teach wisdom [so let it be heard]. But there is [a vital force] a spirit [of intelligence] in man, and a breath of the Almighty that gives men understanding [Prov. 2:6.]. It is not the great [necessarily] who are wise, nor [always] the aged who understand justice. So I say, Listen to me; I also will give you my opinion [about Job's situation] and my knowledge. You see, I waited for your words; I listened to your wise reasons, while you searched out what to say. Yes, I paid attention to what you said, and behold, not one of you convinced Job or made [satisfactory] replies to his words [you could not refute him]. Beware lest you say, We have found wisdom. God thrusts [Job] down [justly], not man [God alone is dealing with him]. Now [Job] has not directed his words against me [therefore I have no cause for irritation], neither will I answer him with speeches like yours. [*I speak for truth, not for revenge.*] [Job's friends] are amazed and embarrassed; they answer no more; they have not a thing to say [reports Elihu] (Job 32:6–15 italics added).

Elihu's discourse about the greatness of God continues for four more chapters. Then the thirty-eighth chapter begins: "Then the Lord answered Job out of the whirlwind," and Job went on to obtain his healing.

It is important to note that God was upset with Job's comforters (42:7), but that Elihu's name is conspicuously absent from the list. What did Elihu do in contrast to that done by Job's comforters? Job's comforters were engaged in the *destructive* use of ignorance for they did not realize their lack of understanding regarding Job's troubles. Elihu shows the *constructive* use of ignorance; realizing he did not know, he took the position of an observer or witness which Christ called us all to be.

By definition, a witness is someone who observes and then reports observations. Yet we have come to believe in Christian circles that a witness is someone who preaches to others. A witness is one who can walk through the valley of the shadow of death with a troubled friend, and by observations discover what factors are related to the distress. If the witness is not blinded by emotional involvement in the illness and has removed the beams from his or her own eyes, the witness will be able to see clearly what caused the illness and what makes it better or worse. Then, together, they can find the pathway out of the valley of despair that will lead to the mountaintop of recovery. Unfortunately, as in the case of Job's comforters, if the blind lead the blind, both will fall into the ditch.

CAUSES OF DEPRESSION

Many approaches could be presented in our attempt to understand depression, but I would like to expand on one model that has been particularly helpful to me in my work with patients with eating disorders.

The word *depression* literally means that something is down or diminished. In a depression of mood, it is difficult to put into words exactly what is diminished, but something such as vitality, drive, or life force is decreased.

Whenever a "down" exists, there must be a reference point against which it can be measured. To have a below sea level, there must be a sea level from which to measure. In my attempt to understand what that measuring point might be in depression, I visualize a reference point based on a person's expectations for his or her performance. A person's expectations are, in turn, based on needs and wants given to us by society and communicated originally through his first and most important teachers, his parents. Much of the pain of depression comes from the disparity between a person's energy level and his expectations, and the greater the distance between them, the greater the pain called depression. Let us take these elements in turn and place them under the observational microscope.

The Interaction Between Drive and Expectation

From birth on, each person is endowed with different levels of drive and energy. In one bassinet lies a youngster who came kicking and screaming into the world and who sleeps little. When this one is fed, he sucks hard and then falls into an immediate but brief sleep. When he awakens with a start, he looks around wondering if he's missed anything. In the next bassinet is the floppy baby who at birth had to be stimulated to even breathe and now seems to sleep continually. Being awakened to eat, and sucking weakly, he falls asleep before the bottle is finished. To some degree these tendencies persist throughout life as is seen in people who function marvelously on four to six hours of sleep and work two jobs with enthusiasm. In contrast is the neighbor who needs nine or ten hours of sleep and who can barely get through an eight-hour-a-day job. Already you may sense your expectations influencing the way you think about levels of drive as you may judge the one needing more sleep as lazy and the one who works two jobs as fulfilling the great American dream.

All of us have fallen into the cognitive trap of believing we are what we do. We can lay this heresy at the feet of René Descartes who said, "I think, therefore I am!" and was acclaimed for his great wisdom. Such a statement cannot be true, for if I did not exist, thinking would be unthinkable; "I am, therefore I think" is more logical as existence must precede function.

Unfortunately, we in Western civilization have carried Descartes' distortion a step further and say, "I do, therefore I am!" thus defining our being by our doing. What question is asked immediately following, "What is your name?" Is it not, "What do you do?"

I always feel compelled to answer, "If I tell you, you won't talk to me anymore," which is good for a fifteen-minute humorous conversation before I reveal my profession. If we were to examine the "I do, therefore I am" statement we would see that it is illogical also; "I am, therefore I do" is the more logical conclusion. This is an important distinction, for it will keep us out of the pharisaical trap of doing good deeds rather than being good people.

We know that a person can do loving deeds, say honest words, and give compassionate responses without being a loving, honest, and compassionate person. But a person who is loving, honest, and compassionate will emit these from the very essence of his or her being.

If people lack energy to do good deeds, many have been taught to feel badly about themselves; even if they would like to do good but can't, they will feel depressed. This is one example of how energy levels, partially determined by genetics, when out of balance with expectations determined by beliefs, can lead to depression.

Any Disease Can Cause Depression

The pastoral counselor may feel that the medical treatment of depression is outside his domain. But I have found that a knowledgeable pastor is often the first to notice the symptoms of depression experienced by a parishioner. He or she may then be the first to suggest that further diagnosis and treatment might be needed. The counselor should be aware that many disease states can cause depression, and it would be useful for the counselor to have at least some familiarity with medicines used to treat depression. This will serve to demystify medical treatment and help the pastoral counselor feel more confident in working with medical members of the treatment team. Furthermore, it is not uncommon for clients to be fearful of medications; the knowledgeable pastoral counselor can play an important part in helping clients work through such fears.

Genetics. If you turn to any standard textbook on internal medicine, you will find that depression frequently appears as a symptom of disease states. Chapters on genetic illness will state that manic-depressive disease runs in families. It is an illness characterized by periods of overstimulation and periods of depression. It requires medical treatment with lithium carbonate (a salt) or sometimes an anticonvulsant medication such as carbamazapine (Tegretol).

Other depressions that do not have periods of overstimulation also run in families, and these tend to respond better to medications such as imipramine (Tofranil), desipramine (Norpramin), amitriptyline (Elavil), or phenelzine (Nardil). Because genetic illnesses have biochemical roots, medical intervention is frequently required.

As most persons with eating disorders have a family history of depression or depression-related illness, medical treatment of depression *must* always be considered.[5]

Metabolism. Biochemical function is very complex and, therefore, it is not surprising that dysfunction can sap one's vitality. It has long been known that an over- or underactive thyroid gland can cause a mood disturbance. Sometimes a treatment-resistant depression is due to a subtle thyroid defect which must be corrected before the depression will respond to treatment.

It has been well established that brain metabolism is impaired in depression. For brain cells to transfer a signal from cell to cell, a number of specific substances are necessary. The transmitter substances in greatest quantity are: serotonin, norepinephrine, and dopamine. These three are made from protein building blocks called amino acids. Serotonin is made from tryptophan; dopamine and norepinephrine are made from phenylalanine.

It is thought that in depression, one or more of the transmitter substances is present in reduced quantities and signals between cells become weak or even get lost. This may explain the mental impairments seen in depression, such as poor concentration, slowed thinking, and memory loss. The reasons for the reduction of the substances may include viral interference with metabolism,[6] endocrine disruption of metabolism, and other unknown causes.

Recently it has been suggested that depression may frequently be caused by a deficiency of the amino acids in the diet.[7] This would explain why persons with eating disorders who may eat inadequate or unbalanced diets deficient in tryptophan and phenylalanine get depressed. It would also explain why clients with anorexia are often unresponsive to antidepressant medication. Due to the starvation diet, deficient in tryptophan and phenylalanine, the basic transmitter substances are not present in sufficient quantities and the medications cannot work without them. This needs to be studied further.

Infections. As we learned from Job's story, depression can lead to infection, but infection can also cause depression. Hepatitis can cause depressive symptoms that may last for a year or more. Mononucleosis typically causes depressions that last from weeks to years, with an average of about six months.[8] I have one client whose mild, chronic hepatitis has contributed to underachievement and aggravated her bulimia, making recovery very slow.

Tuberculosis was noted to have depressive symptoms associated with its chronic course. Indeed, it was while treating tuberculosis with an antibiotic that also affected brain chemistry, doctors discovered depression could be medically treated. Not only did the tuberculosis bacillus die, but the mood of the patients brightened at a surprisingly rapid rate. With the study of this phenomenon, the biochemical factors of depression began to be understood.

Toxins. In medical textbooks, sections on toxicology include a large group of substances labeled depressants. These include alcohol, opiates (including heroin), and sedatives such as phenobarbital and Valium. If you look up phenobarbital and Valium in the PDR (*Physicians' Desk Reference*) you will find depression listed as a side effect.

The use of stimulant drugs, such as amphetamines (speed) and cocaine, will give an initial lift in mood, but it is followed by a rebound depression that can be severe to the point of suicide. The pain of the depression drives the victim back to the drug again and again and addiction results. Many clients with bulimia started with depression induced by the use of appetite-suppressant medication, as they experimented with diet pills in their attempt to control their weight.

Other medications, such as reserpine for high blood pressure and cimetadine (Tagament) for ulcers, can, in some clients, induce depression. When cimetadine is used to treat esophagitis cause by recurrent vomiting, the depression of the bulimic may be aggravated.

Trauma. Trauma can also be a cause of depression, in the debilitating effect of the occurence itself, and in a grief reaction proportional to any permanent loss of function that may have resulted. I have seen a male anorexic whose illness began when a knee injury ended a promising athletic career. Grief from any loss must always be considered as a possible cause of depression. Divorce, death of a parent, or breaking up with a boyfriend are the most common causes that trigger eating disorders.

Cancer. Cancer is a common cause of depression. Its consequences are frightening but there is also evidence that some cancers cause depression by some metabolic mechanism. Cancer of the pancreas often presents itself in this way. Loss of appetite is not uncommon in malignancy or may be induced by its treatment. Not only is nutrition important in the treatment of cancer, but the American Cancer Society has concluded that appropriate diet can play an important role in its prevention. Fortunately, cancer is not an important causative factor in eating disorders, but, with the onset of anorexia nervosa, it is not uncommon for the family and physician to suspect a malignancy before the real diagnosis is discovered.

TREATING DEPRESSION

As we have observed, nearly any illness can cause depression and depression can aggravate many diseases. But conversely, we can improve our vitality and diminish the risk of depression by tending to attitudes and behaviors that lead to optimum health. Health, we know, rests on four legs:

1. Appropriate nutrition
2. Appropriate exercise
3. Appropriate rest
4. Positive mental attitude.

Food as an Antidepressant

The most important antidepressant medication for the anorexic patient is **food.** Without food no one can maintain appropriate metabolic functioning that gives optimum health. But problems arise because the client with anorexia resists taking her medicine.

Some anorexics resist eating because they've discovered that as they lose weight, they experience unusual drive and enthusiasm. Indeed, I know a five-foot-five, eighty-pound woman who was able to run seven miles a day, but as she approached one hundred pounds, her ability to run was diminished, at least temporarily. I believe this curious phenomenon results from an unnatural high, perhaps induced by the outpouring of adrenalin provoked by low blood sugar. I think the anorexic patient can become addicted to this unnatural high, just as the cocaine addict to cocaine, as they both find unhealthy means to fight depression.

I often talk with my anorexic clients about the addictive nature of their illness and remind them that they are really vulnerable if they determine their well-being by how they feel, especially when they are in a euphoric state. James Dobson's book, *Emotions: Can You Trust Them?* is useful in pointing out how feelings are unreliable as the sole source of reality testing. These false beliefs must be challenged by authoritative truth based on objective evidence.

Often the anorexic client will become amenable to treatment only when the starvation state becomes so severe that her weakened body can no longer sustain the euphoria, and participation in any pleasurable activity becomes impossible. As with the alcoholic, the anorexic may have to hit bottom before she is able to turn around. The unfortunate reality is that hitting bottom is physically risky to both the anorexic and the alcoholic; both of these diseases are life-threatening with a significant mortality rate. It is during this bottoming-out, life-threatening phase that medical support and observation are most essential.

The task is to encourage the anorexic to hit bottom as early as possible. On occasion the death of another anorexic can contribute to this turning point. Though it was too high a price to pay, the untimely death of Karen Carpenter helped hundreds of persons with eating disorders to more seriously consider treatment. Following Karen's death, our phones were jammed with calls from frightened people, and attendance at support groups skyrocketed.

Refeeding the Anorexic Client

The refeeding process must be based on gradual increases in calories and in complexity of food. The anorexic eating four hundred calories a day cannot, and usually will not, increase her intake rapidly to two thousand calories a day. Such a change is not only physically unwise but is emotionally unacceptable as well.

For these reasons we encourage clients to increase their caloric consumption by fifty to one hundred calories per day, while providing a great deal of emotional support to overcome the fear uncovered by weight gain. Often the increases seem so small that the client is willing to experiment. We have already discussed the risk of placing undue strain on a weakened heart by overly aggressive refeeding.

To overcome the digestive inefficiency, I suggest easy to digest foods, such as yogurt and soups. Even baby foods are surprisingly well tolerated and received. Vivonex, a liquid food preparation requiring no digestion, is available in "milkshake" form. As the digestion improves, more complex foods can be added as tolerated. A skillful nutritionist's services can be invaluable during this phase of recovery.

Should fear of recovery be too great, hospital care may be necessary to break through the initial hesitation toward refeeding. Because of the fears involved, the "safe" hospital environment with its competent medical staff may be helpful. Even in the hospital, refeeding is only successful if it is coupled with enormous amounts of emotional support from a psychotherapist and/or pastor counselor, as the patient with anorexia finds weight gain extremely stressful and threatening. A mistake sometimes made is to abandon the client to the hospital, feeling all of the needs will be met there. The feelings of rejection that result can undermine otherwise well-designed treatment programs.

While the patient is in the hospital it is too easy for the staff and the patient to focus too much on weight gain and lose sight of the fact that recovery will not be complete until the mood is improved and identity clarified. Five minutes of happiness and contentment is as important a sign of recovery as a pound of weight gain. The visiting counselor may need to keep treatment focused on these other issues.

The Truth that Frees from Depression

Let's turn to the expectational side of the depression equation and continue to explore how unhealthy expectations are based on false beliefs. We have already begun to address these issues in the chapters on perfectionism, low self-esteem, and sexual identity confusion. If the anorexic patient is to participate in a refeeding program, these issues must be included in the treatment plan. It is necessary to explore continually the client's belief system to identify the false beliefs that contribute to the mood problem. Whenever the client gets stuck, one can usually discover a blocking fear based on a false or distorted belief.

For example, a client may attempt to determine her value to the family by observing how strongly the family fights to keep her alive. Other measures of value must be found if she is to relinquish her illness. Others believe that value is determined by appearance, but sex appeal is more than choosing the right toothpaste. Desirability as a human being can be based on values different than grades or income.

Therefore, we must challenge the false illusions about life as presented by television, movies, and the popular press. In real life, people don't get knocked unconscious and then wake up fighting like James Bond. The movies don't deal with realities such as post head-injury syndrome. When television heroes engage in promiscuous sex and never catch herpes or AIDS, viewers are being deceived. When drugs and alcohol are glamorized but liver disease or brain atrophy* are never mentioned, we, the public, are being seduced into false beliefs. When a favorite Western marshal receives serious gunshot wounds during the long run of the program, without his strength and vigor being impaired, a viewer is not being taught about the fragility of life and health.

Ask any police department what its disability rate is and you'll get a clear picture of the truth. Yet we all base many expectations for performance and for life itself upon these "screen" beliefs. Remember, one can do anything in the "funny papers"! Is it any wonder that the anorexic and bulimic clients have a hard time believing they might be permanently damaging their health? Is it any wonder that depression results when the realities presented falsely have such a different outcome in real life, leading persons to feel they are failing to attain the success so magically presented?

The Role of Antidepressant Medications

If depression continues after the anorexic client has attained a healthy weight, which it often does, the employment of typical antidepressant medication must be considered to reduce the risk of relapse. A similar situation exists in the treatment of alcoholism, where alcohol is seen as the depressant. Antidepressant medicines are normally not used during detoxification, as depression usually clears with the removal of the alcohol. Still, some recovering alcoholics will show signs of continuing depression and if the depression is not treated, the risk of relapse is increased. Recent studies show that when a population of alcoholics was released from a detoxification program on lithium carbonate, the rate of relapse was significantly reduced.[9]

I've observed a similar situation in the treatment of anorexia and bulimia. I've seen numerous patients who have been released from behavioral modification programs where the weight was gained and the binging diminished, but they retained their angry, depressed, and sometimes suicidal mood disturbance.

Although many medications have been tried in the treatment of anorexia nervosa, none has shown consistent benefit. Many medicines have helped some, none have helped all. In addition to antidepressants such as amitriptyline (Elavil), antipsychotic medication such as chlorpromazine (Thorazine) and perphenazine (Trilafon) have been used with occasional success, probably because of the antianxiety and antivomiting effects. Other medication such as pimozide, cyproheptadine, lithium, bromocriptine, and naloxone have been used with some success. Because of the seriousness of the illness, if the response to other nonmedical treatment is lacking, several medications may be tried before success is attained.

For bulimia, the story is much more promising. Several controlled and uncontrolled studies show that bulimia is greatly helped in about 90 percent of cases by carefully selecting antidepressant medication.[10] If signs of overstimulation or impulsiveness are present, mood-stabilizing medications are of value. If overstimulation is not present, desipramine (Norpramin) is a relatively safe medication with which to begin. A recent study at the Mayo Clinic using desipramine suggests that many clients with bulimia absorb medication incompletely. A success rate of 90 percent was attained by determining the dose by blood levels of the medication.[11]

There is much more to be done in determining why antidepressants work in eating disorders; and a more systematic method of selection of patients and medication has yet to be determined. When this occurs, treatment will become more effective and efficient.

In summary, treatment of all eating disorders requires a careful evaluation for symptoms of depression and then the development of a plan to deal with the factors present. An appropriate nutrition plan, coupled with appropriate medication, must be prepared and implemented. This must go hand-in-hand with cognitive-behavioral restructuring to modify unrealistic beliefs and expectations. The pastoral counselor is especially well positioned to contribute in the latter area. In addition to Scripture, I use David Burns's book, *Feeling Good,* as major forms of bibliotherapy.

This again points to the need of a collaborative team in treating eating disorders successfully. If it is truth that sets us free, and truth is established in a multitude of witnesses, then there is safety in a multitude of counselors (Prov. 11:14, 15:22, 24:6). It should also be noted that although no approach to the treatment of eating disorders has helped everyone, each has helped someone. Therefore, if your first approach fails, alternative approaches should be sought out and tried. "And let us not lose heart and grow weary and faint in acting nobly and doing right, for in due time and at the appointed season we shall reap, if we do not loosen and relax our courage and faint" (Gal. 6:9).

An Illustrative Case History

One day about seven years ago, a desperate mother and father sat in my office informing me that their daughter had been treated for her anorexia nervosa for nearly a year in a major medical center. She had recently been declared untreatable and was about to be sent to the state mental hospital for "long-term custodial care." They informed me that any objection on their part would be viewed as irrational; the matter would be turned over to Children's Protective Services and the state would obtain custody.

The medical center's treatment had been almost entirely behavioral modification. Occasionally, when their daughter would be allowed to come home, she would sit weeping in her bedroom. But the parents were told not to pay any attention, for such would only reinforce her "infantile acting out."

As I began to acquire a history about the problem, I learned that the illness began within a month of the sudden deaths of both of her maternal grandparents, with whom she had been very close. This had occurred about one year before her first admission to the hospital.

My diagnosis became anorexia nervosa secondary to a pathological grief reaction. I dictated a lengthy letter to the court where her commitment hearing was to be held, outlining the reasons for my diagnosis, coupled with a treatment plan addressing the severe depression. Included in the plan was the recommendation that an antidepressant medication be used to make the pain of the depression less intense. The young girl was fortunate to have a guardian ad litem who took real interest in her problem and who sent a copy of both my recommendations and the recommendations of the medical center to Steve Levenkron, one of the foremost authorities in the field. He recommended the court follow my treatment plan and the judge concurred. Preparations were then begun to transfer the young woman to a hospital where my treatment plan could be carried out.

Because of a three-week wait for an open bed, the medical center elected to begin the antidepressant medication. By the time the patient was transferred, there was already a brightening of her affect.

Her treatment continued to be somewhat stormy, partially because of the lack of trust in the medical profession that had developed in both the patient and her family. The trust began to grow as I compassionately supported the family in their work with their daughter. I asked the mother how she had felt when she had been directed to not comfort her grieving child. She said she felt terrible, and, needless to say, I encouraged her to hold her while she wept bitterly over the death of her dear grandparents. Therapy went through the grieving phases of denial, anger, bargaining, depression, and rebuilding, as described by Kübler-Ross in *On Death and Dying.*[12]

An interesting problem began as we encountered difficulty keeping this patient out of the hospital. She would improve enough to leave, only to regress within two or three weeks after discharge. We carefully examined her hospital experience and noticed she'd formed a strong attachment to an attractive young nurse. Every time she left the hospital and the nurse, her grieving over the loss of her grandparents resurfaced. We asked the hospital if some outpatient contact could be maintained between the patient and the nurse. The hospital objected, fearing they would be held liable should anything go awry. Only after I sent a letter assuming full responsibility under my own insurance, did they finally consent. In the ensuing six months, the girl maintained contact with the nurse by phone and in person, first on a weekly basis and then less frequently, gradually working through the separation. She never required further hospitalization.

After one year in this program, she had attained her full weight, had become more assertive and outgoing, and was able to reestablish herself in school.

This example demonstrates a complete form of antidepressant treatment, including the mix of medication and compassion—someone helping her through the grief process by giving comfort and by following Christ's injunction to weep with those who mourn. Not only were separation fears addressed but her sexual identity was clarified during the rebuilding phase through her identification with a compassionate and attractive nurse. A food plan was provided by the hospital's nutritionist. The fact that her therapist went to great lengths to work out this program let the patient know that she was valued, loved and therefore, lovable—even with her illness. The "long-term custodial care" was avoided and health was regained.

CHAPTER THIRTEEN

TO TELL THE TRUTH
The Deception Factor

A NOTED CHARACTERISTIC of patients with eating disorders is secrecy and deception. Eating, which is normally a social event, becomes a private affair. If the eating disorder victim feels her behavior is socially unacceptable, she carries it out in secrecy. When confronted about such behavior, she denies it, despite the evidence. The anorexic client frequently eats alone; the bulimic binges and purges alone. (When hospitalized and in a situation where common bathrooms are used, the bulimic often stops the purging—temporarily.) Bingers sometimes carry out their dietary excesses between meals or late at night when they ravenously consume the bonbons, breads, and donuts.

Because these are closet illnesses, reliable data pertaining to them is hard to obtain, as it is in any secretive group.

Unfortunately, the dishonesty creates an impasse in the person's life. She often finds it so easy to deceive others that she continually fears she is being deceived. Factual information offered by authoritative people is immediately met with suspicion; the information may be a lie—another attempt to manipulate her. In *Dear Cherry*, a book of letters to and from Cherry O'Neill, one woman says:

> . . . deep down this bothers me because I know I have deceived my family and even my doctor. If I can deceive even my doctor, how can he help me? [1]

Studies show that shoplifting frequently accompanies anorexia and bulimia, the incidence of kleptomania varying from 12 to 24 percent depending on the study.[2] The kleptomania typically involves the shoplifting of food or laxatives, but often includes other nonessentials. Some of my patients have indicated that shoplifting laxatives seemed easier than facing the clerk at the cash register who "must wonder why a person would buy such unusually large amounts." This is often done in spite of the fact that they have more than adequate money to pay for the laxatives. If caught stealing other items, they will nearly always conceal the eating disorder as they go through the complicated procedure of rehabilitation.

Another finding, especially in bulimia, is an unusually high percentage of clients who develop drug or alcohol problems.[3] A casual survey of eating disordered support group participants showed that fully 60 percent of those over age thirty had lost control of their use of alcohol and/or drugs in the attempt to control their eating problems or their moods. This too is generally kept secret, as alcoholics are also noted for the practice of denial. As we have noted earlier, these substances seem to give temporary relief to moodiness, but severely aggravate depression.

MOVING FROM DECEPTION TO TRUTH

The first and most important goal of a counselor dealing with eating disorders is to create an atmosphere in which the illness can be openly examined and dealt with. Indeed, this is the major message of *Dear Cherry*. Anyone struggling with an eating disorder should admit the problem and get competent help. Although this is frequently seen as the patient's responsibility, I believe it is up to the counselor to create the environment where it is safe to tell the truth.

I notice that children, although self-centered, are born without much guile; "out of the mouth of babes comes much truth." In fact, we are often embarrassed by their simple honesty as they, without any deceptive skills, venture into the adult world.

As I see it, deception starts something like this: Mother calls, "Mary, do you have your hand in the cookie jar?"

Three-year-old Mary responds, "Yes, Mother."

Then mother says, "Come here, Mary, I have to spank those naughty hands."

Being a pain-avoiding creature, Mary begins to observe the adult world for clues in how to handle this painful situation. She soon discovers that if she responds with a dishonest no rather than an honest yes, pain can be avoided. And so, generally by the age of six, the little child, exposed to a punitive world, learns to be sneaky and devious like the rest of us.

As I noted earlier, I was once surprised to find that the word *martyr* comes from a Greek word that means "a witness" or "one who tells the truth." Previously I thought it meant "one who died for his or her beliefs." As I further studied the meaning of the roots of the word, I began to understand why the Athenians forced Socrates to drink poison, why Christ was crucified, why Samuel was warned not to return to admonish King Saul, and why contemporary bearers of truth are often met with ridicule and rejection if not outright punishment. Yes, indeed, it is often dangerous and difficult to tell the truth in a dishonest world. Therefore, I can have some compassion for the victims of an eating disorder and some understanding of the deceptive practices. A common statement I hear from these clients is, "I would like to tell the world the truth, but I know the world won't understand." They fear the lack of understanding will lead to rejection and punishment, rather than support and encouragement. John Powell's book, *Why Am I Afraid to Tell You Who I Am?* brings this fear to light.

One of his clients said, "I am afraid to tell you who I am because you may not like who I am and it's all that I have." [4]

Truth Is the Road to Intimacy

Yet we all cry out for intimacy and understanding in our relationship with others. How can I know the truth about you if you can't tell me the truth about yourself? I believe healing cannot occur until the counselor and client have the experience of knowing and accepting each other with regard to a particular problem—what they think and how they feel. Only when this has occurred is there a true emotional bonding between them and the bonding causes the feelings of being separate and alone to be broken down. Until this compassionate encounter has occurred, one cannot feel that his or her burdens are truly shared with another.

In our book, *Marrying for Life,* Dan O'Neill and I defined intimacy as the condition of knowing one another. This requires the sharing of thoughts without reserve. The more intimate we are, the more secure we can feel with each other. In a secure, honest relationship we should begin to feel just as comfortable expressing disappointment, anger, hurt, and frustration as in expressing joy, happiness, success, and pleasure. As I have been pointing out to you, the major obstacle to such free expression is the response of the listener rather than the articulation skills of the speaker. If we are able to hear the pain, and at times even feel the pain, the victim of the illness will be able to "cast their pearls" (his or her most secret, private, and significant feelings) before you without fear of being "trampled in the dirt" (see Matt. 7:6).

Still, the counselor is responsible for responding to the errors of his clients with truth. In David Augsburger's term, "loving enough to tell the truth" [5] requires that we turn away from the gospel according to Emily Post—which has an unwritten rule that if we can't say anything good, we shouldn't say anything at all—and turn to the gospel of Christ which says I must love you enough to tell you the truth. The risk is that truth without love is cruel; love is the spoonful of sugar that lets the medicine of truth be swallowed. If truth is given angrily or harshly it is usually received defensively; if given lovingly and compassionately, it is incorporated into a person's own personality.

Thus, again, the counselor must be a sincere seeker after truth, well aware of his or her own ignorance and deficiencies, so that he or she can humbly apply the constructive use of ignorance. From this we can see the real meaning of Psalm 1: "Blessed is the man who walks not in the counsel of the ungodly, nor stands in the path of sinners, nor sits in the seat of the scornful; but his delight is in the law of the Lord, and in His law he meditates day and night. He shall be like a tree planted by the rivers of water, that brings forth its fruit. . . . whose leaf also shall not wither; and whatsoever he does shall prosper," (NKJV). The law of the Lord referred to is his truth—found in his word and in his works.

Truth from Authority or from Data?

All of us have a hard time establishing what is true and what is false.

We tend to appeal to an authority—whether it be to a parent, scientist, teacher, or a religious prophet. Yet authorities are often wrong. When I first encountered the oral impregnation theory as a cause of anorexia nervosa, I could not find adequate substantiating data even though that theory was touted by authorities of an earlier time. I have come to view ivory towers and gurus with some skepticism, feeling we must be guided by real data rather than by opinion. The Bible says that we shall reap what we sow, implying the existence of cause and effect. It also says we should prove all things and hold fast to those things that prove themselves to be true (Rom. 12:2, 1 Tim. 3:10).

From this comes the scientific model for experimentation. Daniel's experiment, previously mentioned, is a model for any search for truth. For example, when a starving anorexic tells me that she would like to eat more food but becomes gaseous with nausea and bloating after a meal, I believe her. Digestion is often impaired, as previously stated. When I suggest that she eat yogurt or baby food, and when she takes my advice and finds the bloating diminished, I have proven my point. Her experiment has increased her trust in my knowledge.

Often bulimic clients will not believe me when I say that antidepressants might help reduce their tendency toward binging. I sometimes give a two-week sample of the medicines to a skeptical patient, stating that the results should speak for themselves. Eighty percent of the clients are pleasantly surprised with the immediacy of the response. As the tendency toward binging is diminished, trust in the therapist is strengthened. I try to teach the client not to rely on my authority or her authority to establish truth, but to rely on the scientific experiment of trial and error.

I think this is exactly why God does not stop us from sinning, for out of our sinning we do learn the consequences of certain behaviors. If we can confess and repent of our sin we can indeed go and sin no more and avoid the worse things that might befall us. It is the person who hardens his or her heart in the face of truth who continues to flounder in misery. King Saul, for example, paid for the hardness of his heart with the loss of his kingdom and a violent death by suicide. In contrast, David was confronted with the errors of his ways by Samuel and again and again confessed and repented, and never seemed to make the same mistake twice. He was able to turn his errors into learning experiences and, therefore, was called a man after God's heart.

As we become more knowledgeable about the dynamics of eating disorders, we can offer the protection of truth to our clients by predicting the consequences of a continued worsening of their illness. To the anorexic we can say, "If you continue to lose weight, you will become weaker and, in time, your blood pressure will drop. Eventually you will experience fainting episodes, which are usually a sign of cardiovascular weakening. They are an ominous sign that death may not be far away." When the client continues to lose weight and begins to experience the reality of my prediction, credibility and trust are strengthened and she then tends to be more willing to accept medical treatment. *Our task is to tell our clients the truth by clarifying the consequences of their choices, much as Christ did.*

Finally, the Bible says that truth can be "confirmed and upheld by the testimony of two or more witnesses" (Matt. 18:16) and this concept is another one of the pillars upon which modern science stands. If one laboratory conducts an experiment to establish truth, the results are not completely trusted until replicated under similar conditions in an independent laboratory. Fifteen years ago, when I and others stated that depression was a major component of eating disorders, we had little credibility. Now that other centers have presented solid data, it is generally agreed that depression is a cause and must be looked for and treated appropriately if treatment is to be complete.

It is important for the counselor to invite his or her clients to participate in a search for the information upon which recovery will be based. To assist in the search, a reading list is provided in this book (see Bibliography), for as yet no one source of information is adequate to cover the whole subject, and new information is added daily. We have been most successful when the client actively seeks out information about her illness, and applies that information to her unique situation.

Truth Is Clarified by Group Discussion

The biblical principle that truth is established in the company of several witnesses is one of the values of support groups for people with eating disorders. In a group setting, they can share their experiences and through the sharing be guided to the truth. Families of the clients can also benefit both from the information shared and the reduction of the sense of isolation they often feel. The support groups have been most successful when there is a mix of recovered persons and new clients. The beginning clients obviously learn from the experience of those who have recovered, and the recovered find a meaning and purpose for their previous ordeal.

We have used both open support groups and specialized therapy groups with success. The special groups are usually time limited to teach specific skills such as assertiveness, anger management, conflict resolution, and nutrition, to list just a few.

Through all of these efforts we all are guided to the truth that will set victims of anorexia nervosa and bulimia free from the painful ordeal that has bound them.

CHAPTER FOURTEEN

THE POWER STRUGGLE
The Control Factor

EATING DISORDERS GENERALLY OCCUR within action-oriented families, and when the disease finally comes out into the open, either by accident or design, such families generally react with some vigor. Such families face problems with the question, "What are we to do?" rather than, "What is causing this?" Their question leads to actions without adequate understanding, and this in turn may lead to a lack of compliance by family members who do not have confidence that the course of action selected is effective. This usually results in a power struggle between the victim of the illness and the significant others in her life.

In his book *Psychosomatic Families*, Minuchin addresses this issue with paradoxical intention by assigning the family the task of forcing the anorexic patient to eat, which is in effect telling the family to do what they have already attempted.

Of course they soon discover how powerless they all are in dealing with the problem in this manner. The experiment does reveal the weapons that the family uses in its ineffectual negotiations. The battle quickly becomes stalemated with neither side winning—the anorexic patient becoming more firmly bound into her illness, and the family becoming increasingly stuck in frustrated rage.[1] Because of the emotional trauma that results, overt or covert messages are often sent back and forth showing mutual desire for the other party to leave. For example, many parents are willing to pay room and board for the anorexic victim to live apart from the family just to avoid the daily emotional torment. The patient consciously or unconsciously perceives this as an invitation to die.

One of the major weapons used in the power struggle is the ruthless use of guilt in the attempt to gain the upper hand.

The patient may be told that she is "destroying the family," "worrying her mother," "wasting food and money," or "being manipulative and controlling." The compliant side of the patient internalizes this and engages in further self-punishing, self-destroying behavior, much like the rational and irrational behavior of the alcoholic. This only victimizes the family who feels they may have gone too far. Their guilt causes them to attempt to rescue the patient by seeking out new help, buying gifts, or apologizing. The patient, feeling vindicated, may then pounce back on the family by pointing out their errors, attempting to justify her own misconduct by pointing out the misconduct of others. This usually causes the family to revert to the role of persecutor as they defend themselves from this "unjustified" attack. The patient may be attempting to rescue the family from other problems, such as marital disharmony or depression, by distracting the conflict away from those issues and onto herself. In this manner the dynamic of the Karpman Triangle, alluded to in chapter 2, is carried out, all in the attempt to gain control through the unhealthy use of the power of guilt.

Unfortunately, this battle may be unwittingly encouraged by society at large which attempts to reduce socially deviant behavior by provoking guilt feelings with direct or indirect threats of punishment. The church often contributes to this practice, for life-changing religious experiences sometimes do result from a "heart smitten with the guilt of sin." Unless the protection by the message of forgiveness accompanies the message of the "wages of sin is death," the anorexic and the bulimic are left vulnerable to self-destructive urges, and the result may be deadly.

I once received a letter from a pastoral counselor who was working with an anorexic client who was maintaining her low weight by the bulimic behavior of vomiting. He said, "We can see that control is the issue. She is searching for healing, but refuses to follow the family's directions or my directions. She says she likes her anorexia, but not the bulimic behaviors. I felt the place for her to begin would be for her to offer her body to the Lord, and he would enable her to overcome her illness. She is afraid that God wants her fat, because her appetite is so strong. Because she persists in liking anorexia, it seems that nothing can be done for her."

The word *control* and the phrase *refuses to follow directions* are revealing of the power struggle. The client is seen as rebelling against directions of parents and counselor even though the cause of the impasse is revealed in the statement, "She is afraid that God wants her fat."

THE TREATMENT OF POWER STRUGGLES

How does one address this impasse? The counselor is, of course, correct in his belief: If we could live error-free lives, we would reap the benefits. If we could trust God enough to turn our lives over to him, his strength would be made perfect in our weakness. Yet we do what we abhor, and don't do even what we know is best. Thus knowing these general truths is often not sufficient to lead to specific life changes.

Rather than persisting in such an impasse with a client, with everyone involved experiencing a growing feeling of helplessness which soon turns into frustration, I recommend exploring with her the reasons anorexia is appealing.

Why is misery preferable to health? I don't ask, "Why are you choosing death?" but, instead, "Why are you not choosing life?" The answers to that question are always revealing and provide the basis for many therapeutic sessions.

For example, I frequently receive the answers, "My life is miserable. I feel I'll never be good enough to be loved." "I hate myself. If this is all there is to life, why should I choose it?" These responses direct us back to the chapters on perfectionism, low self-esteem, confused sexual identity, and especially, depression. By taking this course, we can avoid the power struggle, and enter into a collaborative exploration of the obstacles that stand in the way of health.

The Problem of Resistance

Early in my psychiatric training, the word *resistance* was commonly used. This brought to my mind the image of somebody digging in his heels, saying, "I bet you can't make me change!"

In years of practice, I learned to see resistance not so much in terms of rebellion, but in terms of fear of change, and of the differentness that would result from change. That's why Eric Berne has said that the therapist really has two main functions: one is to help people see they have permission to change, the second to provide them with protection during the process of change.[2]

Most of us have observed that one who deviates too far from social norms risks rejection. Often, this fear of rejection makes any change difficult. It is, therefore, important that we persuade both the victim of an eating disorder and her family that differences can be seen merely as differences and not as badness to be eliminated by the punishment of rejection.

We must also point out the positive possibilities; differences may be enriching, as new ways of dealing with problems are discovered. When this process is in place, resistance becomes irrelevant as it vanishes in the adventure of living. An example of this is to examine the alternatives to dysfunctional parent-child practices that most of us rely on as parents, alternatives that made the reparenting following a new birth experience so necessary. "If any one comes to Me and does not hate his [own] father and mother [that is, in the sense of indifference to or relative disregard for them in comparison with his attitude toward God] and [likewise] his wife and children and brothers and sisters, [yes] and even his own life also, he cannot be My disciple" (Luke 14:26). As we all have observed, this may lead to differences between people that result in rejection.

Raising Children Without Power Struggles

Many parents are puzzled about the power struggle they have with their children. When children are very young, the behavioral modification techniques of reward and punishment seem to work so well. A slapped hand or paddled bottom seemed to lead to adherence to the family rules. Social isolation—sending the naughty child to her room—was even more powerful, for children would rather be hit than ignored. Still more powerful were the positive rewards of joy, hugs, and gifts in response to accomplishment. Children long remember the joy their parents expressed when hearing their first word or seeing their first step. Surely this encouragement prompts children to learn to talk and walk as early as possible, and guides the child's innate drive for mastery of function.

Unfortunately, later in childhood, such approaches begin to lose their effectiveness. Most parents then try harder, often to no avail. They adhere to behavioral modification despite the approach's loss of power. In *Walden Two*, B. F. Skinner advocates the road to Utopia through the power of reward and punishment, but it was not as effective as hoped for.[3] As his experiment uncovered the difficulties encountered when behavioral modification alone is used in the attempt to create a just society, Skinner, in *Beyond Freedom and Dignity*, called for the restriction of individual freedoms as a necessary step for change.[4] Krutch made impassioned arguments against Skinner's philosophy, warning of its dangers.[5]

Many therapists have attempted to use behavioral modification alone in the treatment of eating disorders with varying degrees of success and failure. When attempts at controlled studies have been made, however, they have shown no evidence that lasting results are accomplished, although the modification certainly can effect a short-term weight gain.[6] It has been my unfortunate observation that when anorexic patients are hospitalized and treated with behavioral modification, they usually gain weight just to get out of the situation. When they are discharged from the hospital they are usually angry, determined to lose the weight rapidly, depressed, and occasionally even suicidal.

Why does behavioral modification lose its power as children grow up? There is really nothing mysterious about it. In the first century, the apostle Paul explained it: "When I was a child, I *talked* like a child, I *thought* like a child, I *reasoned* like a child; now that I have become a man, I am done with childish ways and have put them aside" (1 Cor. 13:11, italics added). Does this Scripture merely mean that when I was a child I played with toys and when I became a man I put my toys away and went to work, never to play again? I think not. The work of Jean Piaget, a Swiss psychologist who studied how the cognitive processes develop throughout childhood, indicates that indeed the thinking, speaking, and reasoning of the child does change as the child matures.[7]

Newborns think in primary process. This type of thinking has two main qualities. First, it is magical, which is why children love cartoons. Second, it is concrete, in that the very young child cannot comprehend cause-and-effect relationships. That's why reasoning with a two-year-old is an exercise in futility. What does work is the behavioral modification of reward and punishment. The statement, "You can't play in the street!" enforced with a paddle is of more benefit than explaining the dangers of an automobile. If the child is too young to even understand the rule, the restriction of a fence or a watchful parent or babysitter provides protection.

Modeling is an even more powerful determinant of human behavior at that age. Because the child learns to walk and open doors before he has good judgment, the most common word heard by a one- or two-year-old is "no!" Because of the power of modeling, the most common word the parent hears from a two- or three-year-old is also the word "no!" which is why this period is called the terrible twos.

Jean Piaget pointed out that at about age three, something amazing begins to happen. Secondary process or abstract thinking begins to develop. It is heralded by the word *why?* and that word is repeated often enough to drive parents to distraction. As children begin to develop the understanding of simple principles of cause and effect, an intense curiosity is aroused. Parents can foster this in hopes that their child will be inquisitive, adventuresome, and, yes, even studious. Too often, however, the curiosity is stifled and repressed as the parent attempts to insist on obedience to the perfect knowledge and wisdom of the family, school, and church. When the child later discovers the imperfections in the parents, teachers, and ministers she can decide to rebel against the behavioral modification programs. This reaction can be seen in the young child who, just after a spanking for violation of the rules, goes right back to the same behavior in spite of the intense tears and pain.

The parent can avoid the loss of influence by protecting the child in the first three years of life with the authoritarianism of behavioral modification. During this period, rules appropriate to the child must be given without explanation. To repeat the example, the two-year-old must hear, "You can't play in the street and if you can't live by that rule, we'll send you to (the jail of) a fenced yard!" At this age, submission to authority is learned.

With the onset of abstract thinking, however, the role of the parent should evolve from that of king to that of teacher. As the child is taught and understands the principle of cause and effect that underlies a specific rule, that aspect of her life can be turned over to her and under the watchful eye of the parent, she can begin to make her own decisions. Thus the authoritarian position of the parent should gradually diminish as his or her teaching role increases. The ultimate goal is not submission to authority but the acquisition of wisdom.

Unfortunately, when behavioral modification begins to lose its power, families usually begin to resort to anger to try to recapture the power. This may give superficial compliance, but under the surface rebellion is sure to begin. It is at this point that we can understand Zechariah 4:6, "Not by might, nor by power, but by my Spirit, saith the Lord of hosts" (KJV).

As the child grows into adolescence, even the anger will lose the effect of superficial compliance, and overt rebellion will be seen. The alternative is to continue in clear and firm teaching as the child grows older. If rebellion does occur it will be against the unchanging laws of nature, as established by God, and explained by the parents. God's laws do not need enforcing; the consequences are built in. To be an effective teacher we must remain in the position set forth in Isaiah 30:15,

"For thus said the Lord God, the Holy One of Israel. In returning to Me and resting in Me you shall be saved; *in quietness and in (trusting) confidence shall be your strength"* (italics added).

During the educational phase of childhood, the goal of wisdom becomes paramount. The importance of wisdom is shown in Proverbs 4:7: "The beginning of Wisdom is, get Wisdom—skillful and godly Wisdom! For skillful and godly Wisdom is the principal thing. And with all you have gotten get understanding—discernment, comprehension and interpretation"; and in 2 Timothy 2:15, "Study and be eager and do your utmost to present yourself to God approved (tested by trial), a workman who has no cause to be ashamed, correctly analyzing and accurately dividing—rightly handling and skillfully teaching—the Word of Truth." Finally, James 1:5 states, "If any of you is deficient in wisdom, let him ask of the giving God [Who gives] to every one liberally and ungrudgingly, without reproaching or faultfinding, and it will be given him."

Piaget goes on to say that the ability to think abstractly, which begins at about age three, rises to the highest level in any given individual at about age thirteen or fourteen. This curiously corresponds with the end of childhood under Jewish tradition. In Christian circles this is the approximate "age of accountability" in which we expect the child to assume responsibility for his or her decisions. Unfortunately, society has invented *adolescence* which stretches from about age thirteen to the age of majority, which used to be twenty-one and has now been reduced to eighteen for most activities except drinking of alcohol.

Too often the child is raised in reverse, permissively when a very young child, but with increasing controls as he or she grows older. Finally as they rebelliously fight their way out of their home, the mutual attitude is, "Goodbye, and good riddance!" This is one environment in which eating disorders flourish.

Be Thankful That Behaviorism Has a Weakness

How wise God was to create us with the ability to think abstractly so we can decide how to respond to a behavioral modification system and thus deprive the system of its power. For example, think of Paul's response to being sent to prison for preaching about Christ. Prison was always meant to be a behavioral modification tool of punishment. Did it work? No. Paul spent the night rejoicing that he could suffer with Christ, and, indeed, his joy influenced many others to follow Christ.

The power struggle is a very difficult problem for many counselors to deal with technically.

When faced with seeming stubbornness, the counselor must be knowledgeable in this area if he or she is to avoid becoming enmeshed in the family impasse. We have already described the nature of the therapeutic personality in chapter 7, and this asset is the beginning point in avoiding the impasse.

In *Treating and Overcoming Anorexia Nervosa*, Steve Levenkron describes the nurturing, authoritative position that is essential in overcoming the illness.[8] Levenkron presents a model for counseling in which the power struggle becomes irrelevant to the relationship between the therapist and the patient. If a counselor knows the principles of cause and effect that are specifically related to the illness, and presents them in a caring manner, the power struggles that take place in the counseling office are between the individual and unchanging reality. Who can rebel successfully against the law of gravity? How can the diabetic attempt to live on cake and still recover his or her health? How can the client with anorexia attain health and joy when she is starving? How can the bulimic safely maintain her weight by vomiting? Remember Galatians 6:7-9:

Do not be deceived and deluded and misled; God will not allow Himself to be sneered at—scorned, disdained or mocked [by mere pretensions or professions, or His precepts being set aside].—He inevitably deludes himself who attempts to delude God. For whatever a man sows, that and that only is what he will reap. For he who sows to his own flesh (lower nature, sensuality) will from the flesh reap decay and ruin and destruction; but he who sows to the Spirit will from the Spirit reap life eternal. And let us not lose heart and grow weary and faint in acting nobly and doing right, for in due time and at the appointed season we shall reap, if we do not loosen and relax our courage and faint.

Paul's own experience with reality is seen in Acts 26:14, "And when we had all fallen to the ground, I heard a voice in the

Hebrew tongue saying to me, Saul, Saul, why do you continue to persecute Me—to harass and trouble and molest Me?" and in Acts 9:5, "It is dangerous and it turns out badly for you to keep kicking against the goad—that is, to offer vain and perilous resistance."

With this in mind, it is my practice to inform the patient and her family that there is nothing that I can do to change the principles of cause and effect. I cannot make an ineffective punitive system work. I cannot bring health to a starving person. Simply trying harder in the behaviors that are currently practiced will just be an exercise in futility and frustration for all of us. Understanding the causes of the illness and finding alternative solutions that have been proven to be effective is the only way for me, the counselor, to provide assistance. In the search for and testing of solutions, I usually try to involve the whole family.

Refocusing Family Energy to Reduce the Power Struggle

Because I find the power struggle usually enmeshed in the eating behavior itself, I attempt to end the family's struggle for control by telling the family members that they are no longer responsible for the eating behaviors. Indeed, I tell them that I will work this out with the patient in individual therapy as we deal with food and weight and the anorexic behaviors of food avoidance, and the bulimic behaviors of binging and purging. I assign the family the task of working with the unhealthy self-esteem, the perfectionism, and the depression.

When a young bulimic soccer goalie burst into tears when she was scored upon, I helped the patient's family and coach respond by pointing out that the ball had to go by ten other players before it even got to the goalie. When she received clarifying support and nurturing comfort, rather than an angry lecture, she relaxed and not only played better but also began to feel confident in her soccer role. This process when generalized into other areas of her life contributed greatly to her recovery.

In such situations my role becomes that of teacher to the family with my objective being to explore the causes of the illness, as discussed in this book. Our success depends on the degree to which we replace the family's frustrated power struggle with an adventure of discovery of new principles and new ideas, which are then incorporated into the beliefs, feelings, and practices of the family.

An important statement directed to the family is that *the patient is not the problem; the illness is the problem.* I remind them that if their daughter had cancer, they would be allying themselves against the illness, seeking out the best care, finding a surgeon who would cut out the cancer, an internist who would poison the cancer, or a radiologist who would disrupt the cancer metabolism with radiation. The patient would receive much support and encouragement to go through such ordeals, and the love and hope so engendered would go a long way in facilitating recovery.

If they say that eating disorders are different because the patient chooses the behaviors that lead to illness, I remind them that there is a growing body of evidence that cancer may also be the result of life-style choices such as smoking, excessive consumption of fat, and the lack of betacarotine foods and foods from the cabbage family in the diet. Too often the person with an eating disorder is seen simplistically as someone who makes bad choices about food, and the complex nature of the disease is rarely considered or understood. I can then persuade the family to side with me and the patient against the illness. In so doing, I have defined my role as a knowledgeable consultant and caring friend rather than a powerful but helpless manipulator and controller.

It is interesting to me that often the family and friends of the patient see the patient as the one who is stubborn, rigid, and rebellious, whereas they define their own position as strength of character, right in their own eyes, and accurate as to what the appropriate solution to the problem is. I usually see things differently. Although outwardly rebellious and inwardly defiant, the patient who comes to my office is often a frightened victim of a potentially fatal illness that is out of control. As her trust in me builds, I find her willing to question her assumptions, beliefs, and practices.

At this point, I often see that the family is more reluctant to participate in the therapeutic change than the ill client. A common initial question that I hear from a family is a subtly defiant, "Tell us, Doctor, where did we go wrong?" Parents usually find my response unsatisfactory. "I do not believe that finding someone to blame is useful. Understanding the process of the illness would be a more fruitful use of our time." At that moment we begin a therapeutic encounter: They are asking me to join them in their belief system involving the rightness or wrongness of behavior; I want to look, without blaming, for the causes that have resulted in an unhealthy child.

If I am successful, I can then guide them through the issues we have discussed in this book, not only in the patient, but in the family as well.

For example, it is my task to point out the contrast between a relationship based on the inadequate definition of love as merely liking and a life based on the definition of love as unconditional, mutual caring. We must point out the destructive results of love earned by achievement only, and challenge the practice of attempting to stamp out failure with punishment, ridicule, and condemnation.

In contrast, we must encourage the family to respond to failure with comfort and encouragement as new methods are found to attain goals. Here past failures are turned into positive learning experiences. We must point out the destructiveness of comparing the patient with healthier brothers and sisters or peers. This eventually teaches the family to accept the client's uniqueness based on their own special mix of strengths and weaknesses.

The Family Is Hurting Too

Because of the genetic quality of the depression in most people with eating disorders, it is important to evaluate other members of the family for mood disturbances as well and suggest treatment for them also. Because of the anger that has often been directed at the patient, depressed parents often fear that equal anger will be directed at them should they admit their own struggle with depression. This, of course, makes it much more difficult for them to accept help. The depressed parent is keenly aware of the response of the counselor to his or her child. It's only when the parent feels comfortable with my approach to their child that the parent will open his or her own problem to effective treatment.

Often parents are quite frightened that if they admit to any error in their belief systems or any personal weaknesses, their children will lose confidence in them and no longer follow their leading. It is helpful to point out that the children already know that their parents are imperfect and have made errors. To pretend otherwise undermines the trust and confidence that children naturally have in adults. Such parents must be shown that an honest statement of "I don't know" often results in greater respect. A better role would be to humbly admit our lack of wisdom, and dethrone ourselves as false gods our children should worship. Instead we must point our children to the true God who is the source of wisdom and knowledge, and the only one worthy of our complete respect and trust.

Who Is Responsible for Deciding?

In working with client and family to clarify choices based on a greater understanding of principles of cause and effect, a difficulty arises as we watch and wait for the client and family to select a course of action that will lead to health. When I see them moving toward an obvious mistake, I am tempted to try to stop them, rather than warn them of expected adverse results and let them decide to see if I am telling them the truth. Christ illustrates the position we must take under these circumstances in his discussion with the rich, young ruler.

. . . Teacher, (You who are essentially and perfectly morally) good, what shall I do to inherit eternal life [that is, to partake of eternal salvation in the Messiah's kingdom]? Jesus said to him, Why do you call Me (essentially and perfectly morally) good? No one (is essentially and perfectly morally) good except God only. You know the commandments: Do not commit adultery; do not kill; do not steal; do not witness falsely; honor your father and your mother. . . . And he replied, All these I have kept from my youth. And when Jesus heard it, He said to him, One thing you still lack. Sell everything that you have and divide [the money] among the poor, and you will have rich treasure in heaven; and come back [and] follow Me. . . . But when he heard this, he became distressed and very sorrowful, for he was rich, exceedingly so. Jesus observing him said, How difficult it is for those who have wealth to enter into the kingdom of God! . . . And those who heard it said, Then who can be saved? But He said, What is impossible with men is possible with God (Luke 18:18–24, 26, 27).

This story suggests that the powerful and the wealthy have difficulty in therapy. Many of them feel, *"If you are so smart, how come you are not wealthy like me?"* With this attitude, it is very difficult for the educated, or the powerful, or the wealthy, or the religious to evaluate their own actions and to modify their own belief systems. Christ's therapeutic response is very interesting, and I believe it is the one we must take in working with both clients and families. His response to the rich man's question not only clarified the choices before him, but also clearly pointed out that the decision was in the rich ruler's own hands. This principle is further illustrated in Matthew 10:11–15:

And into whatever town or village you go, inquire who in it is deserving, and stay there [at his house] until you leave [that vicinity]. As you go into the house, give your greetings and wish it well. Then if indeed that house is deserving, let come upon it your peace [that is, freedom from all the distresses that are experienced as a result of sin]. But if it is not deserving, let your peace return to you. And whoever will not receive and accept and welcome you nor listen to your message, as you leave that house or town shake the dust of it from your feet. Truly, I tell you, it shall be more tolerable on the day of judgment for the land of Sodom and Gomorrah than for that town.

As a therapist, I am here to help clarify people's choices, not to force my beliefs upon them. Christ did not call Peter with his sword to go and make the rich, young ruler follow him. The Matthew 10 passage points out that threat and manipulation are not to be used; a simple clarification of choice is all that is required of me. This must be done with a sense of inquisitiveness, curiosity, and invitation to experiment, rather than with a veiled threat: "If you don't do what I say, you are doomed." We enter into the choice clarification with the attitude of truly proving all things, holding fast to what proves itself to be good. Not only do the family and the patient benefit from this approach, but I have yet to have a patient and family who haven't taught me something new about whatever illness is presented. It is when patience breaks down that counselors resort to manipulative behaviors to try to hasten the therapeutic process. Real growth occurs when we are able and willing to grant the client the time he or she needs to decide which path to take.

For these reasons, when the anorexic patient drops below a safe weight or the bulimic patient begins developing electrolyte imbalance that endangers her cardiac function, I tell her that my fear for her life is destroying my effectiveness as a therapist, for I do not think clearly when I am emotionally upset. I recommend a period of hospitalization until the condition stabilizes. Because I do not do hospital work, such a recommendation involves a referral to other programs in which I have confidence. Knowing that I would not be directly involved in their treatment, the patients themselves often stabilize their own behavior; the weight loss stops or is reversed; the bulimia diminishes and greater care is taken to control electrolyte imbalance. Such a choice enables them to continue to work with me personally. It seems they realize that the issues we have discussed are indeed relevant to their recovery and that mere counting of calories or binges will not be sufficient for recovery. They also understand my message that I cannot choose their behavior; I can only choose my own. To those who have been involved in power struggles with others, this release from that struggle is a relief. We can then focus on more relevant issues. As their condition stabilizes, we are able to adapt the Alcoholics Anonymous philosophy of "one day at a time" to "one step at a time" and explore the many facets of the issues that we are presenting in this book.

Potential Power Struggles in the Office

I find that some issues can lead to power struggles between counselor and patient, including the issue of whether or not the client will get on the scale and be weighed at weekly sessions. Anorexic clients especially fear losing control of situations, or even sharing control, and are, on occasion, reluctant to get on the scale in the presence of the counselor. If they appear to be quite tenuous in weight or have symptoms of cardiovascular decompensation such as fainting episodes, it is essential that I have accurate data to estimate the current degree of danger. Even at less critical times, the objective measure gives us, at least physiologically, some indication whether or not the therapy is making any difference. Almost all patients will allow me to measure their blood pressure, both sitting and standing, and if it is unusually low (below 90/50), I can then more strongly emphasize the need to get on the scale.

If then, in my clinical judgment based on visual observation, I believe the client is at significant risk and her life in danger, I will tell her that unless we can determine her weight, there is little reason to continue outpatient therapy, for treatment is not something that I do to her but with her. We must work together. If I do not make it an issue, there is no way that she can feel that I truly care for her and about her recovery. Unless she can receive my care, I, as a therapist, will have little influence in her life.

If the patient's health is not critical, I often take parts of two or three sessions to resolve the issue about weighing. The result is a situation in which the patient's curiosity about therapy becomes our ally as she, too, wonders whether what we do will be effective when so many other approaches she has tried previously have failed. As recovery begins I often observe an ambivalence toward progress. On one hand she feels a satisfaction in knowing that her progress can be *measured* and not merely felt. On the other hand, the patient's anxiety over weight gain is often quite intense, requiring me to comfort, encourage, and support her through the stress of change.

Payment May Be a Therapeutic Tool

Another potential power struggle occasionally surfaces in the area of payment for services. For the compulsive anorexic client, this is rarely a problem, but it is more likely to occur in the treatment of bulimia. Bulimia is an expensive illness. The cost of food consumed can exceed six hundred dollars per month. I have had clients who cashed their medical insurance checks, used part of the funds to binge and purge, and then claimed they couldn't pay their full bill. I handle this with straightforward honesty: "A servant is worthy of his hire."

As my definition of love is "caring about someone else's well-being and security as much as I care about my own," I discuss the fact that I must care about myself, so that I, in turn, can care about them. The concept of mutual concern must be in place as part of the recovery process; how the client handles the bill is indicative of her willingness to participate in a life based on the law of love. I sometimes remind patients that the payment of a bill, although important to my well-being, is not essential, for 95 percent of my clients do handle their accounts responsibly and this is more than enough for my needs. Handling of the bill irresponsibly will only increase their sense of guilt, thereby lowering their self-esteem further and making their recovery more difficult. Sometimes the family also uses this area of money to discover how I respond to potential power struggles.

I once worked with the family of the vice-president of a large corporation who began to underpay his account significantly. When I questioned him about this, he said that he was only concerned with paying bills where interest was charged for delinquency and, inasmuch as physicians do not charge interest, my bills did not have very high priority to him. In response, I reminded him that my well-being did not totally depend upon his payments to me, but that his well-being certainly did, for his attitude was a statement to his wife and child about the value he placed on their health. I was also puzzled that a man who had such an attitude toward contractual obligations could rise to such a position of responsibility.

Curiously within a month of our conversation, this man was released from his job. After several months of unemployment he frantically approached his previous employer who hired him back, but at a position several levels below his previous job. When that happened, he wrote me a letter offering to pay back the bill in full. But, because his income had been cut by 75 percent, his payments would have to be somewhat modest. I obviously agreed to that and, although it took two years, he paid the entire account. When his daughter saw his new, responsible, caring attitude, she was able to invest herself more heavily in therapy and make a good recovery.

Power Struggles Over Medication

Another potential power struggle involves the use of antidepressant medications in the treatment of bulimia. Some people insist that they want only "natural treatment." If such clients have symptoms of an agitated, restless depression suggestive of a bipolar mood disorder and I think lithium carbonate might be effective, I point out that lithium carbonate is not, by any definition, a drug per se. It is a mineral salt like sodium chloride in the salt shaker on their table. I encourage them to read Ronald Fieve's book, *Moodswing,*[9] which points out some of the apparent benefits of living in an area where the drinking water is rich in lithium salts. Finally, to set up the experiment and peak their curiosity, I will offer them a week's supply of lithium and suggest they begin the experiment if and when they would like. Every client I have approached in this way has taken the mineral and, if my clinical judgment is accurate, benefited as well.

When patients realize that I will not and cannot force them to take medication against their will, they usually become more receptive to the experimental approach. At that point other medications can also be offered. In order to get a smooth response and reduce the risk of side effects, I often begin antidepressant medication at very low doses, sometimes as low as one-tenth the expected therapeutic dose and gradually work it up as tolerated. With this approach, the patients see me as a fairly conservative physician who indeed wants them to have a good response but is willing to make the changes gradually. This helps them overcome their fear of recovery and also their fear of losing control, which is ultimately the core of the power struggle.

Teaching the Family to Resolve Power Struggles

Special conflict-resolution training is often required for the family. The goal of such training is for all family members to see conflicts as a problem to solve rather than a contest to win. In John 14:27 Christ said, "Peace I leave with you; My [own] peace I now give and bequeath to you. *Not as the world gives do I give to you*"(italics added). As I try to understand what this statement means, I notice that the world only knows two ways of pursuing peace. The first is the hawkish approach; people arm themselves and attempt to obtain peace by conquering their foes. In the family situation, parents attempt to cure the anorexic or bulimic daughter with anger, threat, and punishment. The other approach is that of the dove; a person surrenders his or her position and loses the contest by default. It could be argued that Neville Chamberlain, who surrendered Poland in the name of peace, only whetted the appetite of the hawkish Hitler.

Perhaps we should look for other birds in the woods besides hawks and doves. Having spent ten years in the military, I devoted a significant portion of my life to the study of war. I came to the conclusion that when we prepare for war, we certainly do not bring peace; but neither do we bring peace when we take the position of the helpless dove.

Christ gave us the solution to conflict in Matthew 18:15, 16: "If your brother wrongs you, go and show him his fault, between you and him privately. If he listens to you, you have won back your brother. But if he does not listen, take along with you one or two others, so that every word may be confirmed and upheld by the testimony of two or three witnesses." This clearly states the first approach to conflict resolution: privately go to the person with whom you disagree and try to establish where both sides of the river are so a bridge can be built. Too often a person sees only one viable position, his or her own. Anyone who differs from that person is simply wrong. We needlessly spend our time throwing rocks across the river rather than seeing how the rocks could be used to build a bridge.

An example of this impasse is seen in the couple who considers their anorexic daughter bad and weak-willed; although the daughter may agree that she is bad, she knows she is not weak-willed, as she has a powerful control over her weight. A small, healthy part of most anorexic clients with whom I have worked recognizes that their behavior is "sick" and unhealthy. In this situation the therapist must help the parents who see their daughter's illness as a weakness to begin to value the strength of her resolve, even though the strength is put to unhealthy use. The daughter needs help to see that the hurt and anger which her parents experience come from real, heartfelt concern, for if they didn't truly care they would just let her die without a word. My role is to function as a witness to help them clarify both banks of the river, to assist in the bridge-building of compassion, and to end the rock-throwing.

At this point families don't need a judge to determine who is right or wrong, nor do they need a counselor to tell them precisely what to do. They literally do need a witness, one who, by definition, observes and reports observations. From those observations, solutions to the conflict can be found. Once the bridges are built, the power struggle ends. This is accomplished neither by the hawkish nor the dovish approach, but by looking for solutions that are loving and fair to all involved. Thus again I am teaching the family to live under the law of love in which solutions, to the best of our ability, meet the needs of every family member. Perhaps that is what Paul meant in his letter to the Ephesians, "Be subject to one another out of reverence for Christ, the Messiah, the Anointed One" (5:21).

The power struggle becomes irrelevant when the counselor forms a collaborative relationship with clients, when their mutual goal is to gain an understanding of truth about the multiple factors of the problem. When truth is pursued with a sense of adventure and discovery, solutions can be found, and these solutions can be selected freely after they have been put to the test of reality and experience.

There is a time when, to save a life, the decision about treatment cannot be left to a severely ill victim of anorexia nervosa. Through the involuntary Treatment Act of the State of Washington, I have on only two occasions had to elicit the support of the courts in insisting on treatment when patients were so clearly irrational and near death that they could not make a reasonable choice to stay alive. Not every state will insist that patients with eating disorders be treated involuntarily. Where it is allowed it can be implemented only in extreme cases and only by physicians or by specially trained counselors designated by the courts, although anyone can request the proceedings. It is generally much better to obtain voluntary cooperation of the patients by establishing a close working relationship.

CHAPTER FIFTEEN

MISS PETER PAN
The Dependency Factor

IT IS NOT SURPRISING THAT A PERSON who sees herself as a failure, with seemingly uncontrollable behaviors, would look to others for control yet resist control because she has been taught to value autonomy and freedom. This leads to a condition of hostile dependency which has been present, to varying degrees, in the clients with eating disorders with whom I have worked.

Classic psychoanalytic theory has observed hostile dependency among patients with manic-depressive disease who have extreme difficulty with impulse control. Such patients often seek out a strong, limit-setting and challenging therapist with whom they battle. They attempt to persuade the therapist that their grandiose plans are nothing short of creative genius. They look to the therapist to save troubled marriages, cancel unwise business transactions, and rescue them from the police and the courts when their behavior crosses the boundaries of the law. Yet they will often angrily oppose questions or statements used to dissuade them from impulsive actions.

I can recall vividly the six-foot-three, 240-pound manic patient assigned to me during my first year of residency training. On Fridays he would angrily demand a weekend pass; if I did not grant it, he said he would throw me out of the fifth-floor window. I steeled myself and stated, "When you ask for a pass in that manner, it is proof that you are not ready." He would say, "Okay," turn on his heel, and walk away. He needed me to be strong enough to set limits, but he didn't like it.

The alcoholic who has tried many measures to control his or her drinking without success may try to persuade a spouse to take charge of the alcoholic's behavior. Bottles are hidden, angry lectures are given, threats are frequently yelled. When that fails, the alcoholic involves the police, employers, and friends in the pursuit of control. I've already alluded to the Karpman Triangle, a three-positional, interactional pattern of persecutor-victim-rescuer that serves to maintain the hope that someone else will rescue the alcoholic from uncontrolled drinking.

EATING DISORDERS AND FAMILY RESCUE

When we focus on eating disorders, we often observe the same pattern as in alcoholism. The impulsive bulimic woman will sometimes marry a controlling, critical man, hoping her fear of him will help her resist her impulsiveness.

We have noted how the persecutory role provokes perfectionism while damaging self-esteem. We have also shown how the persecutory role is used in the attempt to gain control in the power struggle. In all cases, it is fairly easy to see that all are victimized by the process.

In the attempt to provoke the family to control her abusive eating habits, the bulimic will often binge on foods prepared for the evening banquet. If a mother sets aside food for the exclusive use of her bulimic daughter, she will eat that and the family stores as well. If a family sets aside a bathroom for exclusive use of the bulimic member, it will sometimes be left as a smelly mess which cannot be long ignored. Excessive consumption of family resources through the "waste of food," and kleptomania, which causes the family embarrassment, may also fit this pattern. One can see that the bulimic patient is victimizing her family through persecutory behaviors.

When the family retaliates with harsh, firm rules, such as, "If you want to eat, you'll have to earn your own money," or when the family criticizes and condemns, they move into the role of persecutor and the bulimic wife or daughter becomes the victim. In this role, the anorexic or bulimic patient vigorously engages in self-punitive behaviors such as excessive exercise, rigid dieting, and/or increased binging and purging. As a result, her health deteriorates. Symptoms such as fainting, muscle spasms, weight loss or the other signs of physical deterioration previously described will eventually occur. When this happens, the family, feeling guilty for their harshness, will revert to the role of rescuer and the cycle begins again. Unfortunately, when the family attempts to rescue their victim daughter, they foster dependency by implying that they can take responsibility for her behavior.

Sometimes the roles are split with the father being a critical persecutor, the mother being the protective rescuer, and the patient floundering in confusion about which role to be in. An example is the family in which the father literally moved out of the house, stating that the daughter's illness had become more important to the family than was his own well-being. He did, however, continue to support the family financially and visited often. The mother hovered over the patient, offering food, encouragement, and medication in order to keep her daughter alive. The daughter felt responsible for breaking up the family, the guilt aggravating her depression; yet she enjoyed being the recipient of her mother's concern and loving attention. The daughter was trapped in the situation where she was both punished by her father and rewarded by her mother for the same behavior.

In other situations, the client's attempt to become independent is subtly undermined by her own family and thereby the illness is unconsciously being reinforced. These patterns from a behavioral standpoint must be identified and modified if there is to be success. For example, I have encountered the depressed, divorced (or widowed) father who financially rewards his daughter for continuing to be sick so that she cannot grow away from him and expose him to a second loss he fears he would not survive. Many times the patient unconsciously recognizes this and attempts to protect her father from his pain (even suicide) by sacrificing her own health and future life. Such a situation usually leads to hostile dependency on the part of the young woman who, at some level of awareness, is struggling with the unfairness of her plight.

The solution is to compassionately identify the father's fears and assist him with his own depression. Through his improved mental health, he can give up his daughter to her own destiny and receive back the love of a healthy, happier, better-adjusted woman and, one hopes, in time, the eventual affection of a son-in-law and grandchildren.

People severely ill with an eating disorder are afraid to grow up for fear they will handle the responsibilities of adulthood as poorly as they handle their own health. Most women with bulimia are able to hold responsible jobs, just as most alcoholics do. Because of the constant torment of their illness, bulimic women do, however, lack the complete joy and satisfaction they deserve. If one looks closely one can generally find either obvious or subtle behavior aimed at encouraging someone else to take charge of the out-of-control aspects of her life.

The person with anorexia often attempts to arrest her psychosocial development in a much earlier phase; she rejoices at her flat chest, lack of periods, and the fact that she is not troubled by boyfriend problems. In anorexia nervosa, a twenty-seven-year-old woman can have the physical characteristics of a prepubertal child. As health is slowly regained, anorexics express much anxiety about the developing breasts, the return of periods, and the interest of men. They are often concerned about having to deal with boyfriend problems because they feel they do not handle those very well. Frequently, there is an unspoken feeling that *If my parents really loved me, they would not expect me to go out into the cold, cruel world but would take care of me always.* Just like Peter Pan, they are trying to live in Never-Never Land and they hold to that fantasy world with great tenacity.

ARE WE OUR BROTHER'S KEEPER?

Clarification of the problem of dependency came to me through an encounter with a wise and respected rabbi, a friend of my first partner in my practice. On occasion, Rabbi Raphael Levine would eat lunch with us, and one day he turned to me and said with a twinkle in his eye, "The trouble with you Christians is that you think you are your brother's keeper!"

I said, "Yes, Rabbi, I think you are right."

He asked where I thought that philosophy came from, and I replied that it came from the Book that his ancestors wrote. He acknowledged that was true and asked if I knew what part of the Book.

I said, "Yes, the story of Cain and Abel in Genesis."

He nodded and asked me how the story went.

I said, "Well, after Cain killed Abel, and God asked Cain where Abel was, Cain asked God the famous question, 'Am I my brother's keeper?' "

Rabbi Levine then asked, "And how did God answer the question?"

My mind went blank as I couldn't remember the answer. He invited me to get my Bible and look it up, which I did. To my amazement, I found that God didn't answer Cain's question.

Rabbi Levine said, "To us Jews, that's an important part of the story for we believe there is no single answer to the question." He continued, "Dr. Vath, I understand you've just had a son born to your house, and I know you will be a good father, providing for all of his needs."

I smiled proudly and acknowledged that this was true.

But then he asked me what I would think of myself if I were still providing for him in the same way when my son was fifty years old.

I replied, "I would have destroyed him!"

And he asked, "What will you have to do between now and then to ensure that that outcome does not occur?"

After some thought, I said, "I will have to learn to say no to him, for if I carry him too long he will not learn how to walk."

This conversation changed my whole attitude about charity

and giving. I try to state the truth I learned in this way: *We must do for others what they cannot do for themselves, but we must not do for them what they will not do for themselves. The problem is finding the wisdom to know the difference.*

How many spoiled children have been raised by mothers who have been overly self-sacrificing? How many lives have been destroyed by unwise social welfare programs? Perhaps Solomon was correct when he said that there is a time to give and a time to receive, that there is a time and place for everything under the sun. Giving must be balanced by receiving.

RAISING CONFIDENT CHILDREN

One reason growing up is difficult is because most children are raised somewhat backwards. In the previous chapter, I defined the need in early childhood for the parent to be controlling and authoritarian, gradually changing to a less authoritarian, teaching role as the child grows older and wiser. This would suggest that parents gradually transfer responsibility from the parent to the child over an eighteen to twenty-five-year period. Too often parents have done the reverse, being permissive when the children are young, and increasing their authoritarian control as the children grow older. By the time children are ready for emancipation, the parents are making the most important decisions for them. When the children finally do leave home, they often leave without much confidence in their ability to choose wisely; therefore, it is no great surprise to us when they fail.

In light of this, one of the responsibilities of parenthood is to raise children who are wise rather than merely submissive and obedient. This does not happen overnight, but should happen over the multi-year period, when they are taught the skills of decision-making and problem-solving from data rather than opinion only. Children must learn to choose the wise solution rather than what feels good or what feels right.

TEACHING CLIENTS TO ASSUME RESPONSIBILITY

As we apply this philosophy to the treatment of eating disorders, we must understand how to help people become successes rather than failures. Success is defined as the attainment of a goal. Therefore, a life without goals is devoid of success. Together with our patients we must set clear goals and then teach our patients how to attain these goals in a stepwise manner. Every major goal is attained through the accomplishment of intermediate steps that are, in reality, short-term goals themselves. In doing this we must help them change their approach from an all-or-nothing thought pattern to seeing that the longest journey can be broken down into smaller, manageable steps.

An example of this can be seen in the patient who was vomiting eleven to twelve times a day. At first I asked her to keep a record of how many times she binged and purged each day. I didn't mention that either of us would attempt to change the frequency. Our beginning to count the number of episodes helped her begin to modify her behavior, and within two weeks the pattern was reduced by nearly half. This gave us an opportunity to rejoice over a partial success, pointing out that binging and purging only six or seven times a day was indeed an improvement over the eleven or twelve times that had been occurring prior to this experiment. By doing this we were also able to associate the change in the binge and purge syndrome with events in her life, noticing that depression, discouragement, and conflict tended to cause a rapid and sudden increase in the frequency of binging. This then led to a phase of therapy that focused on stress-coping skills so that the difficult situations could be handled in healthier ways than by binging.

An example of this occurred as we discovered the binges were associated with recurrent depression. When we provided her with effective medication, her depression left and the binging and purging stopped. Under this circumstance we are offering the patient an internal, biochemical method of gaining control of seemingly uncontrollable behavior.

Cherry O'Neill talks about this in her book, *Starving for Attention,* noting that within two weeks after she was started on lithium she felt a growing sense of being in control.[1] Once the controls are felt to be real and powerful, people who have looked for external control tend to relax and expect less control from others. Suddenly the external controls seem less necessary or desirable. In a related situation, recent studies show that the use of lithium carbonate for alcoholics recently discharged from detoxification centers significantly reduces the recidivism rate in that impulse-control disease also.[2]

When effective treatment is offered and the client feels she is beginning to regain control of her impulsive, self-destructive behavior; when she is able to set goals more realistically and see success within her grasp, she can then feel as though she can be freed from her golden cage and enter into the meaningful life of responsible adulthood. The satisfaction of performing a job well can then be tasted; a close, intimate relationship developed and maintained. It is only then that the person with a previously out-of-control eating disorder can experience what Paul wrote about in Galatians 6:4, "But let every person carefully scrutinize and examine and test his own conduct and his own work. He can then have the personal satisfaction and joy of doing something commendable [in itself alone] without [resorting to] boastful comparison with his neighbor."

By following the principles that we have outlined in this book, which are merely the attempt to clarify God's natural laws as they apply to eating disorders using the scientific method of proving all things, our clients can enter into the freedom that Christ promised. "So if the Son liberates you—makes you free men—then you are really and unquestionably free" (John 8:36).

CHAPTER SIXTEEN

HEALTHY LIVING

THERE IS A BOOK FOR ADOLESCENTS that has a great title: *If You Don't Know Where You're Going, You'll Probably End Up Somewhere Else,* by David Campbell. Without clear goals, our lives become fragmented and disorganized. Life becomes reactive to circumstance rather than self-directed. We become victims of fate rather than masters of our destiny. This is also true in therapy, which can become disorganized and direction-less unless both the counselor and the client develop clear goals to be attained.

Initially it is important for the goals to be clear to the counselor, but if they are introduced too early to the perfectionist client, she can be overwhelmed. The client may drop out of treatment as she views such an "impossible" task. Initially it is useful to talk in general terms, such as "We want you to be healthy and trim, rather than sickly and thin," but as therapy progresses, more specific goals must be introduced. After all, is not the attainment of a long-term goal made up of short-term goals that are consistent with the long-term goal?

SIGNS OF RECOVERY

I am indebted to a colleague, a recovered bulimic and now therapist, Dr. Kim (Lampson) Reiff, for developing the following list of criteria for recovery. She presented these in February 1984 at a symposium on anorexia nervosa and bulimia at Providence Medical Center in Seattle, Washington. When you are establishing goals for therapy, you'll want to keep these criteria for recovery in mind. It is important to realize that recovery is a developmental process that continues throughout a patient's lifetime. Recovery is not like running across a finish line, after which struggles and problems disappear.

Acceptance

A sign of recovery is the ability to recognize and accept the imperfections of self and others. No longer will self-worth be determined by the attainment of unrealistically high performance standards. Instead, a client must learn to accept herself and others as human beings who possess a complicated mixture of strengths and weaknesses that lead to some successes and some failures. She must learn to rejoice with the success and skill of others and with her own success and skill as well. She must learn to comfort others at their points of weakness and failure, just as she needs comfort.

Love of Self and Others

As part of the resolution of the perfectionism dilemma, a client's self-esteem is greatly improved; she shifts from external to internal qualities as the source of worth. As people learn that performance and achievement are not the measure of self-worth; as they turn to the three learnable skills of love, honesty, and compassion (as goals to strive for, not as rules to be obeyed), an unflappable self-worth can develop. A person committed to those eternal values can not only feel good about herself but can and will ultimately receive more and more accolades as she demonstrates to others her faithfulness.

As the client works through her relationship with authority figures, a deeper and meaningful relationship with God will result. As she perceives God's nature more accurately as a loving, guiding Father, she will welcome his participation in her life. With such a relationship with the Source of love, her self-worth can be eternally established.

Appropriate Womanliness or Manliness

As part of improved feelings of self-worth, it's important for the client to develop a valuable and functional and comfortable concept of sexual identity. When the client has attained this, it is easy to see him or her living out the various aspects of his or her sexual and social role with confidence and with assertiveness. For example, as menstruation returns to the anorexic woman, it is important that she face this without embarrassment and perceive it as a natural and normal function of a woman.

Joy

It is important that the depressive aspects of the illness be significantly ameliorated so the client generally has vitality, energy, and a reasonable joy for the present and hope for tomorrow. She also should have the ability to tolerate those occasional rainy days and blue Mondays that everyone experiences.

Open Honesty

As self-acceptance grows, she will be both comfortable and confident in sharing her successes with humility and her failures without shame. She will seek out others who respond with the empathy and compassion that result from honesty tempered by love. This will result in close, lasting friendships that hold fast during the stormy times of life.

Independence

The client who sees the disorder as a problem to be solved rather than a sin or a mistake to be hidden is well on the way to recovery. This allows her to pursue wisdom for life rather than answers to specific questions. Wisdom will lead her to a self-directed autonomy that can conquer many problems, whereas the pursuit of answers to questions makes her dependent upon authority figures for her continual well-being. This does not mean that the opinions of others should not be considered but that they should be evaluated, tested, and then incorporated into the person's life only if they prove to be helpful and based in reality.

Collaboration

As a result of all of these improvements, the client's approach to life becomes self-assured. She will negotiate openly and freely with others, demonstrating confidence. For example, the person with an eating disorder should be able to maintain a reasonably stable weight that is close to the body weight set point without anxiety. Such practices include habitual, confident selection of healthy foods, a reasonable plan of exercise and rest, all under the umbrella of a confident attitude. This healthy attitude includes the lack of panic over sudden fluid shifts, the ability to eat an occasional dessert in moderate amounts without panic, the ability to overeat periodically without fear and with a confident resumption of normal eating practices following such an episode.

When these thoughts, feelings, and behaviors are present to a reasonable degree and when they have become a very part of the individual's personality, one can be reasonably sure that the eating disorder has been resolved. The longer the new behaviors continue, the more they become part of the individual's nature and less the possibility of relapse. This will enable the person to live confidently knowing that the illness has died so that the client can live. The prisoner of this illness is now free as its bonds have been broken.

CHAPTER SEVENTEEN

FREE AT LAST!

AFTER BECKY HAD RELATED HER STORY, I responded that the story was familiar to me and that the many issues of eating disorders were present. I handed her my list of issues and without my help she quickly began to associate sequences from her story that fit them. Yes, she could see her perfectionism in her academic strivings and her desire to win approval from others. The fact that she felt unsuccessful in spite of acknowledged successes suggested that her self-esteem was indeed impaired. The issue that brought her to my office, her new boyfriend, had revealed the lack of confidence in her identity as a woman. She sincerely wanted this clarified. The hours spent in the despair of depression were recalled with feeling.

My Kleenex box provided essential tools as her tears flowed freely. Her story was full of the many attempts to conceal her illness, and again, it was her fear of discovery that drove her to my office for help. In Becky's case, the family was not overtly coercive in the attempt to get her eating under control, but the bribes and guilt-inducing statements were seen as subtle forms of the same process. With her eating behaviors still uncontrolled, she felt she could never live totally independently for she felt she needed the fear of rejection to assist her wavering ability to control her appetite. Previous periods of successful control generally followed the supportive pressure of others, or the fear of discovery by others.

In the first family session, I shared my list of issues that would have to be faced, and as usual, the family readily recognized the relevance of each to the family. They seemed relieved that the illness could be understood in this way. Breaking the problem down into its smaller parts seemed to make it less threatening. They were even more relieved when I asked them to turn over the problem of weight and eating behavior to Becky and myself to resolve. I stated that the areas they could be most helpful in the recovery process would be in the treatment of perfectionism, low self-esteem, and sexual identity confusion. Becky's father especially welcomed the opportunity to help validate her femininity by expressing his approval more directly. In no time, Becky's relationship with her family improved.

I explained that we would together design a treatment plan for each issue, and that the completeness of success would depend on how well we could come up with a plan for each issue. We then began to look together at perfectionism as we started at the top of the list. I shared with Becky the Four Vath Rules and suggested that she review them daily until she believed them. I suggested, for example, that she leave a period off the end of a term paper to see what the response would be. Later, it surprised her to find it was not missed by her hurried professor and she received a good grade.

We also suggested that she begin to count her bulimic episodes to establish a base line so that as interventions were made we could determine if they were truly effective. She reported that her bulimia was not constant, but variable with days that were free of binging; on the whole she was binging three to four times a week. During the two weeks she was counting, she noticed that the second week was free of binging totally, but the third week resulted in a relapse. I reminded her that even that was an improvement, that practice did make better.

We then discussed her moodiness and she agreed to try a period of antidepressant medication as control of her bulimia could be more rapidly attained. She was then started on a low dose of desipramine (Norpramin) and the dose was increased to full therapeutic levels over a week's time. One week later she reported a significant drop in her cravings for sugar; her mood became joyful as irritability vanished. As the binging ceased, time for other activities was readily available. Needless to say, Greg became an increasing part of those activities.

After two months of treatment, Becky wondered if it would be necessary to share her problem with Greg. I asked how serious she was about this relationship, and she responded that she hoped it would last forever. I asked how a forever relationship could be possible if a wedge of a secret problem would keep them apart forever. Was it important to discover if Greg's love was sufficient to love her even if she was imperfect?

She saw the value of this and over the next two weeks gradually broke the news to Greg that she was consulting a psychiatrist. As that did not seem to deter him, she decided to share the nature of the problem with him and invite him to a joint session. Greg, wanting to help the woman that he had come to love dearly, welcomed the chance. He stated that if there was anything he could do to help, he was committed to do it. I suggested that the eating aspects of the problem were not of major concern for him, except the need to accept Becky's limits on food portions. "No need to push the second piece of cake, huh!" he stated. I shared with them both the ingredients of a healthy relationship—love, honesty, and compassion—and suggested they experiment with these concepts. Successes as well as failures were shared. Each found that when caring love was strong, failures were comforted and success met with rejoicing.

In dealing with Becky's guilt over her past, we discussed with her the biblical teaching about forgiveness. She decided to check out my statements with her pastor, saying that I really wasn't a minister, even though my initials are REV! When her pastor confirmed the belief that sins are forgiven when presented with confession and repentance, she was doubly assured. She felt clean and whole again, able to face the world without the load of guilt. She and Greg began to attend church regularly as they began to think of the source of traditional family values.

As the next month progressed, Becky began to blossom. Her face radiated her joy, her demeanor confidence, and her behavior enthusiasm. Even her family commented on the change. We all felt that the power of love played a major role in this transformation, but Becky knew that the control of the bulimia also helped.

After six months without relapse, we began to taper Becky's medication. This was first met with some anxiety as Becky discovered she was giving all the credit to her recovery to the medication and not enough credit to her changing attitudes. Still there was sufficient trust in me to attempt this successfully.

Soon Becky and Greg graduated from college, and by that time were inseparable. Four months later I received an invitation to their wedding, which was not a real surprise to me, having watched the relationship grow, almost from its inception. At this time we began to terminate treatment, reducing sessions to once a month. After six such visits without a sign of relapse, therapy was concluded. Becky does know that she is somewhat vulnerable to depression, however, and asked me to keep my door open should the signs ever recur.

It has now been three years, and I have not seen Becky professionally, but meet her on occasion in the community. Of course, her story is necessarily brief, undoubtedly making recovery sound too simple. Still if you recall that the issues Becky, Greg, and I discussed have been covered in this book in some detail, you will see that the treatment was complete and therefore successful.

CHAPTER EIGHTEEN

IF IT'S SOMEONE YOU KNOW

A COMMON QUESTION ASKED of counselors is "What do you do if you know of someone with an eating disorder, especially if that person is reluctant to acknowledge the problem?" As in alcoholism or drug abuse, the first challenge is to get the person victimized by an eating disorder to admit that the disease exists. How the counselor responds to this question reveals much about his or her approach to therapy in general and will determine whether or not such evasive patients will ultimately be engaged in therapy.

The first answer to this "How do I help a friend" question is: Prepare yourself by gathering as much information about the problem as you can. This is exactly what Al Anon does for the friend of the alcoholic. Read some of the books in the bibliography included in this book. Then call the associations for eating disorders, also listed, as they provide referral services, names and addresses of effective therapists, and treatment programs. If a friend has gathered information about the illness, he or she has jumped a major hurdle in creating an atmosphere in which help is apt to be accepted.

After a friend has taken the time and energy to gather information he or she can then approach the person with the eating disorder. Always express concern for the individual and not criticism. This is a painful illness, and compounding the pain only reduces the likelihood of acceptance of help. The most powerful message is, "I care about you and have demonstrated it by the lengths that I have gone to in attempting to find help for you." If one recalls the story of the Prodigal Son, it was not the father's prosperity or his sermonizing that brought the prodigal home. It was the recollection that there was love in his father's house. So it must be with a friend of a person with an eating disorder. It is also important to realize that the first encounter may not be successful, but, if love is indeed patient and longsuffering, multiple messages will be sent.

When a victim of an eating disorder finally acquiesces to the continued invitations of a concerned friend, it is important to select an appropriate counselor. The concepts outlined in this book can be used as a measuring stick to determine whether or not the counselor possesses the insight and the personality characteristics essential for recovery.

Some people are more willing to go to counseling if a friend is allowed to accompany them to at least the first visit. Most family counselors and those who value collaborative effort would accept this, whereas others may not. At least offer to accompany the individual, again supporting the importance of the decision to do something about the problem. If the counselor has been checked out beforehand, it is likely that the referral will be successful. If personality clashes do occur and movement is not made in a reasonable time, it is not unwise to seek out another therapist with whom the client might be more compatible.

Often the patient with the problem perceives referral as rejection. To avoid this, it is important to stay in the relationship with the victim to the degree possible, as continued support and encouragement are very helpful in guiding the ill person to a healthy recovery. If support groups are available in your community, you might accompany the struggling friend to the meetings. There are many steps along the path to recovery that are frightening, overwhelming, and discouraging. These hurdles are more apt to be made successfully when there is a supportive friend to add encouragement and comfort along the way.

APPENDIX 1

1983 Metropolitan Height and Weight Tables

TO MAKE AN APPROXIMATION OF YOUR FRAME SIZE. . .

Extend your arm and bend the forearm upward to a 90 degree angle. Keep fingers straight and turn the inside of your wrist toward your body. If you have a caliper, use it to measure the space between the two prominent bones on *either side* of your elbow. Without a caliper, place thumb and index finger of your other hand on these two bones. Measure the space between your fingers against a ruler or tape measure. Compare it with these tables that list elbow measurements for *medium-framed* men and women. Measurements lower than those listed indicate you have a small frame. Higher measurements indicate a large frame.

Height in 1″ heels Men	Elbow Breadth
5′2″—5′3″	2½″—2⅞″
5′4″—5′7″	2⅝″—2⅞″
5′8″—5′11″	2¾″—3″
6′0″—6′3″	2¾″—3⅛″
6′4″	2⅞″—3¼″
Women	
4′10″—4′11″	2¼″—2½″
5′0″—5′3″	2¼″—2½″
5′4″—5′7″	2⅜″—2⅝″
5′8″—5′11″	2⅜″—2⅝″
6′0″	2½″—2¾″

HEIGHT AND WEIGHT TABLES

Weights and ages 25-59 based on lowest mortality. Weight in pounds according to frame (in indoor clothing weighing 5 lbs. for men and 3 lbs. for women; shoes with 1″ heels).

MEN				WOMEN			
Height Feet Inches	Small Frame	Medium Frame	Large Frame	Height Feet Inches	Small Frame	Medium Frame	Large Frame
5 2	128-134	131-141	138-150	4 10	102-111	109-121	118-131
5 3	130-136	133-143	140-153	4 11	103-113	111-123	120-134
5 4	132-138	135-145	142-156	5 0	104-115	113-126	122-137
5 5	134-140	137-148	144-160	5 1	106-118	115-129	125-140
5 6	136-142	139-151	146-164	5 2	108-121	118-132	128-143
5 7	138-145	142-154	149-168	5 3	111-124	121-135	131-147
5 8	140-148	145-157	152-172	5 4	114-127	124-138	134-151
5 9	142-151	148-160	155-176	5 5	117-130	127-141	137-155
5 10	144-154	151-163	158-180	5 6	120-133	130-144	140-159
5 11	146-157	154-166	161-184	5 7	123-136	133-147	143-163
6 0	149-160	157-170	164-188	5 8	126-139	136-150	146-167
6 1	152-164	160-174	168-192	5 9	129-142	139-153	149-170
6 2	155-168	164-178	172-197	5 10	132-145	142-156	152-173
6 3	158-172	167-182	176-202	5 11	135-148	145-159	155-176
6 4	162-176	171-187	181-207	6 0	138-151	148-162	158-179

APPENDIX 2

NATIONAL DIRECTORY OF SOURCES FOR HELP

ANRED
(Anorexia Nervosa and Related Eating Disorders)
P. O. Box 5102
Eugene, Oregon 97404

National Anorexic Aid Society
P. O. Box 29461
Columbus, Ohio 43229

NAANAD
(National Association of Anorexia Nervosa and Associated Disorders)
P. O. Box 271
Highland Park, Illinois 60035

American Anorexia Nervosa Association, Inc.
133 Cedar Lane
Teaneck, New Jersey 07666

BIBLIOGRAPHY

First and foremost, I recommend *The Amplified Bible*, published by Zondervan (1965). This version has been particularly helpful to me, in that it does "not attempt to give a word-for-word translation, but only aims at the sense of the original author's idea."

The second book to read should be Larry Crabb's *Effective Biblical Counseling*, also published by Zondervan (1977). This book gives a method we can use to analyze the complex and sometimes contradictory information obtained through secular study. If such information does not make it through the "sieve" of the Bible, be careful, as the Bible is undoubtedly the correct position.

Finally, I recommend that those books marked with the symbol * be read next, as they contain current basic information about eating disorders and their treatment. Although we now know more about this topic, there is still much more to be discovered. New information is published monthly in medical journals which can be obtained from your local county medical association.

BOOKS

Augsburger, David. *Caring Enough to Confront*. Ventura, Calif.: Regal Books, 1980.

* Berne, Eric. *What Do You Say After You Say Hello?* New York: Grove Press, 1972.

Bloom, Lynn; Coburn, Karen, and Pearlman, Joan. *The New Assertive Woman*. New York: Delacorte Press, 1975.

Bruch, Hilde. *Eating Disorders: Obesity, Anorexia Nervosa, and the Person Within*. New York: Basic Books, 1979.

————. *The Golden Cage: The Enigma of Anorexia Nervosa*. Cambridge: Harvard University Press, 1978.

* Burns, David. *Feeling Good*. New York: William Morrow, 1980.

Chernin, Kim. *The Obsession: Reflections on the Tyranny of Slenderness*. New York: Harper and Row, 1981.

Dally, Peter, and Gomez, Joan. *Obesity and Anorexia: A Question of Shape*. New York: Harper and Row, 1980.

Dobson, James. *Emotions: Can You Trust Them?* Ventura, Calif.: Regal Books, 1980.

* Fieve, Ronald. *Moodswing*. New York: William Morrow, 1975.

Flach, Frederic. *The Secret Strength of Depression*. New York: Lippincott, 1974.

* Garner, David, and Garfinkel, Paul (eds). *Handbook of Psychotherapy for Anorexia Nervosa and Bulimia*. New York: Guilford Press, 1985.

Glasser, William. *Reality Therapy*. New York: Harper and Row, 1965.

Levenkron, Steven. *The Best Little Girl in the World*. New York: Warner Books, 1979.

* _____. *Treating and Overcoming Anorexia Nervosa*. New York: Scribner's, 1982.

Menninger, Karl. *Whatever Became of Sin?* New York: Hawthorn, 1973.

Minuchin, Salvador, et al. *Psychosomatic Families: Anorexia Nervosa in Context*. Cambridge: Harvard University Press, 1978.

O'Neill, Cherry. *Dear Cherry*. New York: Continuum, 1985.

* _____. *Starving for Attention*. New York: Continuum, 1982.

Palazzoli, Mara. *Self Starvation*. New York: Jason Aronson, 1978.

Palmer, R. L. *Anorexia Nervosa: A Guide for Sufferers and Their Families*. New York: Penguin, 1981.

* Pope, Harrison, and Hudson, James. *New Help and Hope for Binge Eaters*. New York: Harper and Row, 1984.

Powell, John. *Fully Human, Fully Alive*. Niles, Ill.: Argus, 1976.

_____. *Why Am I Afraid to Tell You Who I Am?* Allen, Tex.: Argus, 1969.

* Satir, Virginia. *Conjoint Family Therapy*. Palo Alto, Calif.: Science and Behavior Books, 1967.

Smedes, Lewis. *Forgive and Forget*. New York: Harper and Row, 1984.

Steiner, Claude. *Games Alcoholics Play*. New York: Random House, 1977.

* Vath, Raymond, and O'Neill, Daniel. *Marrying for Life*. Minneapolis: Winston, 1982.

Vincent L. M. *Competing with the Sylph: The Pursuit of the Ideal Body Form*. New York: Berkley Books, 1981.

* Vredevelt, Pam, and Whitman, Joyce. *Walking a Thin Line*. Portland, Ore.: Multnomah Press, 1985.

ARTICLES

Barchas, J., Akil, H., Elliot, G., Holman, S., and Watson, S. "Behavioral Chemistry: Neuroregulators and Behavioral States." *Science* 200 (1978): 964–973.

Connors, M., Johnson, C., and Stuckey, M. "Treatment of Bulimia with Brief Psychoeducational Group Therapy." *American Journal of Psychiatry* 141(1984): 12:1512–1516.

Drinkwater, B. "Bone mineral content of amenorrheic and eumenorrheic athletes." *New England Journal of Medicine* 311(1984): 277–281.

Faust, I. "The Role of the Fat Cell in Energic Balance Physiology." *Psychiatric Annals* 13(1983): 843–851.

Free, N., Green, B., Grace, M., Chernus, L., and Whitman, R. "Empathy and Outcome in Brief Focal Dynamic Therapy." *American Journal of Psychiatry* 142(1986): 917–921.

Garner, D., Garfinkel, P., and O'Shaughnessy, M. "The Validity of the Distinction Between Bulimia With and Without Anorexia Nervosa." *American Journal of Psychiatry* 142(1985): 581–587.

Gold, P., Gwirtsman, H., Augerinos, P., Nieman, L., Gallucci, W., Kay, W., Jimerson, D., Ebert, M., Rittmaster, R., Loriaux, L., and Chrousos, G. "Abnormal Hypothalamic-Pituitary-Adrenal Function in Anorexia Nervosa: Pathophysiologic Mechanisms in Under-weight and Weight-Corrected Patients." *New England Journal of Medicine* 314(1986): 1335–1342.

Halmi, K. A., Eckert, E., LaDu, T., and Cohen, J. "Anorexia Nervosa: Treatment Efficacy of Cyproheptidine and Amitriptyline." *Archives of General Psychiatry* 43(1986): 177–181.

Hecht, H., Fichter, M., and Postpischil, F. "Obsessive-compulsive Neurosis and Anorexia Nervosa." *International Journal of Eating Disorders* 2(1983): 69–77.

Heymsfield, S., Bethel, R., Ansley, J., Gibbs, D., and Felner, J. "Cardiac Abnormalities in Cachectic Patients Before and During Nutritional Repletion." *American Heart Journal* 95(1978): 584–594.

Hsu, G. "The Treatment of Anorexia Nervosa." *American Journal of Psychiatry* 143(1986): 573–581.

Jaret, P. "The Wars Within." *National Geographic* 169(1986): 702–735.

Johnson, C. "The Etiology of Bulimia: A Bio-psycho-social Perspective." *Annals of Adolescent Psychiatry* 13(1985).

Johnson, C., and Flach, A. "Family Characteristics of 105 Patients With Bulimia." *American Journal of Psychiatry* 142(1986): 1321–1324.

Karpman, S. B. "Script Drama Analysis." *Transactional Analysis Bulletin* 7(1968): 39–43.

Keesey, R., and Corbett, S. "Metabolic Defense of the Body Weight Set Point." *Psychiatric Annals* 13(1983): 838–841.

Kerndt, P., Naughton, J., Driscoll, C., and Loxterkamp, D. "Fasting:

The History, Pathophysiology, and Complications." *Western Journal of Medicine* 137(1982): 379–399.

Lindberg, J. "Exercise Induced Amenorrhea and Bone Density." *Annals of Internal Medicine* 101(1984): 647–648.

Powers, P. "Heart Failure During Treatment of Anorexia Nervosa." *American Journal of Psychiatry* 139(1982): 1167–1170.

Rigotti, N. "Osteoporosis in Women with Anorexia Nervosa." *New England Journal of Medicine* 311(1984): 1601–1606.

Rubenstein, E. "Diseases Caused by Impaired Communication Among Cells." *Scientific American* 242(1980): 102–121.

Stunkard, A. "Eating Disorders: Obesity Introduction." *Psychiatric Annals* 13(1983): 835–838.

Swift, W., Andrews, D., and Barklage, N. "The Relationship Between Affective Disorders and Eating Disorders: A Review of the Literature." *American Journal of Psychiatry* 143(1986): 290–299.

Walsh, T., Stewart, I., Roose, S., Gladis, M., and Glassman, A. "Treatment of Bulimia with Phenylzine." *Archives of General Psychiatry* 41(1984): 1105–1108.

Warren, M., Brooks-Gunn, J., Hamilton, L., Warren, L., and Hamilton, W. "Scoliosis and Fractures in Young Ballet Dancers: Relation to Delayed Menarche and Secondary Amenorrhea." *New England Journal of Medicine* 314(1986): 1343–1347.

Wurtman, R. and Wurtman, J. "Nutrients, Neurotransmitter Synthesis, and the Control of Food Intake." *Psychiatric Annals* 13(1983): 854–857.

NOTES

Chapter 2   Eating Is a Complex Activity

1. Proceedings of the Conference on the Decline in Coronary Heart Disease Mortality. U.S. Department of Health, Education and Welfare. Public Health Service. DHEW Pub. No. (NIH)79–1610.

2. J. Stamler, "Population Studies" in R. I. Levy (ed), *Nutrition, Lipids and Coronary Heart Disease* (New York: Raven Press, 1979), 25–88.

3. Hilde Bruch, "Four Decades of Eating Disorders" in David Garner and Paul Garfinkel (eds), *Anorexia Nervosa and Bulimia* (New York: Guilford Press, 1985), 17.

4. Alyson Hall, "Outpatient Group Treatment" in David Garner and Paul Garfinkel (eds), *Handbook of Psychotherapy for Anorexia and Bulimia* (New York: Guilford Press, 1985), 250.

5. S. B. Karpman, "Script Drama Analysis," *Transactional Analysis Bul* 7(1968): 39–43.

6. Claude Steiner, *Games Alcoholics Play* (New York: Random House, 1977).

Chapter 3   Diagnostic Criteria

1. American Psychiatric Association: *Diagnostic and Statistical Manual of Mental Disorders—III* (Washington, D.C.: American Psychiatric Association, 1980).

2. Ibid.

3. H. Hecht, M. Fichter, and F. Postpischil, "Obsessive-compulsive Neurosis and Anorexia Nervosa," *International Journal of Eating Disorders* 2(1983): 69–77.

Chapter 4   What Eating Disorders Do to the Body

1. J. Isner, QT Interval Prolongation in Anorexia Nervosa, Report to the 56th Session of the American Heart Association.

Chapter 5   Appetite Control

1. Nathan Pritikin, *The Pritikin Permanent Weight-Loss Manual* (New York: Bantam, 1981).
2. Robert Haas, *Eat To Win* (New York: Rawson, 1983).
3. A. Stunkard, I. Thorkild, C. Sorensen, T. Teasdale, R. Charkraborty, W. Schull, and F. Schulsinger, "An Adoption Study of Human Obesity." *New England Journal of Medicine* 314(1986): 193–198.
4. Clara Davis, "Feeding After the First Year," in J. Brannemann (ed), *Practice of Pediatrics*, Vol. 1 (Hagerstown, Md.: W. F. Prior, 1957), chap. 30.
5. R. Wurtman and J. Wurtman, "Nutrients, Neurotransmitter Synthesis and the Control of Food Intake," *Psychiatric Annals* 13(1983): 854–857.
6. E. Rubenstein, "Diseases Caused by Impaired Communication Among Cells," *Scientific American* 242(1980): 102–121.
7. I. Faust, "The Role of the Fat Cell in Energic Balance Physiology," *Psychiatric Annals* 13(1983): 843–851.

Chapter 6   The Effects of Starvation

1. A. Keys, J. Brozek, A. Henschel, O. Mickelson and M. Taylor, *The Biology of Human Starvation* (Minneapolis: University of Minnesota Press, 1950).
2. David Garner and Paul Garfinkel (eds), *Handbook of Psychotherapy for Anorexia Nervosa and Bulimia* (New York: Guilford Press, 1985), 523–532.
3. Keys, et al., 833.
4. R. E. Fritch, "Fatness and Reproduction: Delayed Menarche and Amenorrhea of Ballet Dancers and College Athletes," in P. L. Darby (ed), *Anorexia Nervosa: Recent Developments* (New York: Alan R. Liss, 1983), 343–364.
5. P. Powers, "Heart Failure During Treatment of Anorexia Nervosa," *American Journal of Psychiatry* 139(1982): 1167–1170.

Chapter 7   Social Perception Versus Reality

1. A. Toufexis, "Dieting: the Losing Game," *Time* 20 Jan 1986, 53–60.

2. C. Johnson, C. Lewis and S. Love, "Incidence and Correlates of Bulimic Behavior in a Female High School Population," *Journal of Youth and Adolescents* 13(1984): 15–26. R. C. Casper, E. Eckert and K. A. Halmi, "Bulimia: Its Incidence and Clinical Significance in Patients with Anorexia Nervosa," *Archives of General Psychiatry* 37: 1030–1035.

3. K. A. Halmi, J. Falk and E. Schwartz, "Binge-eating and Vomiting: A Survey of a College Population." *Psychiatric Medicine* 11: 697–706.

4. J. D. Killen, "Self-Induced Vomiting and Laxative and Diuretic Use Among Teenagers," *Journal of the American Medical Association* 255(1986): 1447–1449.

5. A. Toufexis.

6. Ibid.

7. John Adams Atchley, "At 64, Some Thoughts on Bulimia, Psychiatry, and the Practice of Medicine." Lecture at B.A.S.H. meeting in Oct. 1984.

Chapter 8   Helping the Helper

1. J. Verloff, R. A. Kulka and E. Dovran, *Mental Health in America: Patterns of Help Seeking from 1957–1976.* (New York: Basic Books, 1981).

2. R. Mollica, F. Streets, J. Boscarino and F. Redlich, "A Community Study of Formal Pastoral Counseling Activities of the Clergy," *American Journal of Psychiatry*, 143:6: 323–328, (Mar. 1986).

3. Carl Rogers, *On Becoming a Person* (Boston: Houghton Mifflin, 1961), 39–58.

4. Harry Stack Sullivan, *Conceptions of Modern Psychiatry* (New York: W. W. Norton, 1953), 42, 43.

5. Corrie ten Boom, *The Hiding Place* (Old Tappan, N.J.: Revell, 1974), 215.

6. David Augsburger, *Caring Enough to Confront* (Ventura, Calif.: Regal Books, 1980), 1.

7. Albert Ellis, *Reason and Emotion in Psychotherapy* (New York: Lyle Stewart, 1962).

8. Aaron Beck, *Cognitive Therapy and the Emotional Disorders* (New York: New York University Press, 1976).

9. David Burns, *Feeling Good* (New York: William Morrow, 1980).

10. Steve Levenkron, *Treating and Overcoming Anorexia Nervosa.* (New York: Scribner's, 1982), 20–25.

Chapter 9 The Best Little Girl in the World

1. Cherry O'Neill, *Starving for Attention* (New York: Continuum, 1982), 158.
2. Allan Nevins, *John D. Rockefeller: The Heroic Age of American Enterprise, Vol 2* (New York: Scribner's, 1940), 427, 428.
3. Levenkron, *Treating Anorexia Nervosa*, 8, 9.
4. Mao Tse-Tung, S. B. Griffin, trans., *On Guerrilla Warfare* (New York: Praeger, 1961), 25.
5. *Encyclopedia Americana*, "Religion," Vol. 16, 1985.

Chapter 10 The Worst Little Girl in the World

1. Thomas Harris, *I'm OK—You're OK* (New York: Harper and Row, 1969).
2. Eric Berne, *What Do You Say After You Say Hello?* (New York: Grove Press, 1972), 147–156.
3. Karl Menninger, *What Ever Became of Sin?* (New York: Hawthorn Books, 1973).

Chapter 11 What Is a Woman?

1. William Glasser, *Schools Without Failure* (New York: Harper and Row, 1969).
2. Eugene Bliss, "Anorexia Nervosa," in *Comprehensive Textbook of Psychiatry/II* (Baltimore: Williams and Wilkins, 1975), 1657.
3. Harrison Pope and James Hudson, *New Help and Hope for Binge Eaters* (New York: Harper and Row, 1984).
4. J. Hudson, P. Laffer, and H. Pope, "Bulimia Related to Affective Disorder by Family and Response to Dexamethazone Suppression Test," *American Journal of Psychiatry* 139: 685–687.
5. C. Johnson, and R. Larson, "Bulimia: An Analysis of Mood and Behavior," *Psychosomatic Medicine* 44: 333–345.
6. Mary Ellen Pinkham, *Mary Ellen's Help Yourself Diet Plan* (New York: St. Martins, 1983).
7. Haas.
8. E. Flick, "Nutritional Aspects of Magnesium Metabolism," *Western Journal of Medicine*, 133: (Oct. 1980).

9. J. Kobayashi, "On Geographical Relationship Between the Chemical Nature of River Water and Death Rate from Apoplexy," *Ber Ohara Instituts Lanwirschafliche Biol.*, 11 (1957): 12–21.

10. D. R. Taves, "Fluoridation and Mortality Due to Heart Disease," *Nature* 272(1978): 361, 362.

11. E. B. Dawson, "Relationship of Lithium Metabolism to Mental Hospital Admission and Suicide." *Diseases of the Nervous System* 33: 1972.

12. E. W. Burney, "Basic and Clinical Studies of Endorphins," *Annals of Internal Medicine* 91: 239, 1979.

13. Berne, 120–122.

14. Raymond Vath and Daniel O'Neill, *Marrying for Life* (Minneapolis: Winston Press, 1982), 44.

Chapter 12   To Be or Not To Be

1. O'Neill, 128–150.

2. Cherry O'Neill, *Dear Cherry* (New York: Continuum, 1985), 121, 122.

3. Nathan Kline, *From Sad to Glad* (New York: Ballantine, 1974).

4. S. J. Schleifer, S. Leller, M. Camerino, J. Thornton and M. Stein, "Suppression of Lymphocyte Stimulation Following Bereavement," *Journal of the American Medical Association* 250(1983): 374.

5. J. Hudson, H. Pope and J. Jonas, "Family History Study of Anorexia and Bulimia," *British Medical Journal* 142(1983): 133–138.

6. P. Southern, "Medical Consequences of Persistent Viral Infection," *New England Journal of Medicine* 314(1986): 359–367.

7. M. Sabelli, J. Fawcett, F. Gustovsky, J. Javiad and P. Wynn, "Clinical Studies on the Phenylethylamine Hypothesis of Affective Disorders: Urine and Blood Phenylacetic Acid and Phenylalanine Dietary Supplements," *Journal of Clinical Psychiatry* 47(1986): 66–70. S. Cole, "L-Tryptophan: Clinical Studies," McLean *Hospital Journal* 5(1980): 37–71.

8. S. Straus, G. Tosato, G. Armstrong, T. Lawley, O. Preble, W. Henle, R. Davey, G. Pearson, J. Epstein, I. Brus and M. Blaese, "Persisting Illness and Fatigue in Adults with Evidence of Epstein-Barr Virus Infection," *Annals of Internal Medicine* 102: 7–16, 1985.

9. D. Fawcett, "Evaluation of Lithium Therapy for Alcoholism," *Journal of Clinical Psychiatry* 45(1984): 494–499.

10. H. Pope, J. Hudson and J. Jonas, "Bulimia Treated with Imipramine: A Placebo Controlled, Double Blind Study," *American Journal of Psychiatry* 140: 554–558. 1983. T. Walsh, J. Stewart, S. Roose, M. Gladis and A. Glassman, "Treatment of Bulimia with Phenelzine: A Placebo Controlled, Double Blind Study, *Archives of General Psychiatry* 41(1984): 1105–1109. R. Horne, "Buproprion in the Treatment of Bulimia," unpublished.

11. P. Hughes, L. Wells, C. Cunningham and P. Ilstrup, "Treatment of Bulimia with Desipramine," *Archives of General Psychiatry* 43(1986): 182–186.

12. Elisabeth Kübler-Ross, *On Death and Dying* (New York: Macmillan, 1969).

Chapter 13   To Tell the Truth

1. O'Neill, *Dear Cherry*, 103.

2. R. Casper, E. Eckert, K. A. Halmi, S. Goldberg and J. Davis, "Bulimia: Its Incidence and Clinical Importance in Patients with Anorexia Nervosa," *Archives of General Psychiatry* 37(1980): 1030–335.

3. Harrison Pope and James Hudson, *New Help and Hope*, 57.

4. John Powell, *Why Am I Afraid to Tell You Who I Am?* (Allen, Tex.: Argus, 1969).

5. David Augsburger, *Caring Enough to Confront* (Ventura, Calif.: Regal Books, 1980).

Chapter 14   The Power Struggle

1. Salvador Minuchin, et al. *Psychosomatic Families: Anorexia Nervosa in Context* (Cambridge: Harvard University Press, 1978).

2. Berne, *Transactional Analysis in Psychotherapy* (New York: Grove Press, 1961), 123–125, 371–376.

3. B. F. Skinner, *Walden Two* (New York: Macmillan, 1948).

4. B. F. Skinner, *Beyond Freedom and Dignity* (New York: Alfred A. Knopf, 1971).

5. J. W. Krutch, *The Measure of Man* (Indianapolis: Bobbs-Merrill, 1954).

6. K. A. Halmi, P. Powers and S. Cunningham, "The Treatment of Anorexia Nervosa with Behavioral Modification," *Archives of General Psychiatry* 32: 93–96.

7. Jean Piaget, *The Development of Thought: Equilibration of Cognitive Structures* (New York: Viking Press, 1977).

8. Levenkron, *Treating Anorexia Nervosa*, 8.

9. Ronald Fieve, *Moodswing* (New York: William Morrow, 1975).

Chapter 15 Miss Peter Pan

1. O'Neill, *Starving for Attention*, 146.

2. D. Fawcett, "Evaluation of Lithium Therapy for Alcoholism," *Journal of Clinical Psychiatry* 45(1984): 494–499.

INDEX

Activity, starvation effects on, 20, 21, 52–54

Admission indications for inpatient treatment of anorexia, 22–24, 138

Alcoholism and eating disorders, 30–31, 146

Anorexia nervosa: behavioral therapy, 157, 161; obsessive-compulsive traits, 38; cognitive therapy, 80, 101; diagnostic criteria, 36–38; medical treatment, 22–24, 137, 140, 142, 172; self-help and support groups for, 151

Antianxiety agents in therapy, 140

Anticonvulsants in eating disorders, 42, 134, 142

Antidepressants in eating disorder treatment, 134, 140–142, 170, 179

Anxiety of weight gain, 138–139

Appetite control, 46

Atchley, John Adams, 59

Attitudes: effects of starvation on, 52–53; of treatment staff toward patients, 23–24, 63

Augsburger, David, 70, 148

Autonomy: family role, 174–176; therapy of, 177–180

Beauty, social standards, 57, 58, 116

Beck, Aaron, 71

Behavior: cognitive effects on, 71, 95–97; starvation effects on, 52–54

Behavioral therapy in eating disorders, 157, 161

Beliefs, 71, 80, 95–98, 101

Berne, Eric: critical parent, 106; parental influence on identity, 121–122; role of counselor, 156

Bible references on: child development, 158; cognitive therapy, 71, 106; compassion, 73, 94; condemnation, 71, 106; conflict resolution, 89; correction, 90; counseling, 63, 73, 76–77; depression, 128–131; freedom, 180; love, 67–69, 75, 84; perfection, 83–84, 91, 98, 104; power, 87, 159; punishment, 86–87, 106; repentance, 105–106; responsibility, 166–167; suffering, 74; wisdom, 104, 160

Bibliotherapy, 118, 141, 170, 197–198

Body image, 20, 57, 58, 88, 116, 117

Body weight set point, 49–50

Bone loss in anorexia, 42

Bruch, Hilde, 30

Bulimia: cognitive treatment, 80, 101; complications of, 42–44; diagnostic criteria, 36–38; family therapy, 112–114, 156, 164–165, 176; medical treatment,

Raymond E. Vath, M.D.

Raymond E. Vath is a psychiatrist with an M.D. degree and psychiatric training from the University of Washington. He has published several scientific articles in professional journals and has coauthored with Dan O'Neill, *Marrying for Life.* He has contributed to the work of others including Pat Boone's *Coming Out,* and Cherry O'Neill's *Starving for Attention.*

Dr. Vath is in private practice in Bellevue, Washington, is a clinical assistant professor of psychiatry at the University of Washington, and a visiting professor at Seattle Pacific University. He is a board member of Mercy Corps International, and a popular speaker in religious, academic, and professional organizations.

He lives in western Washington with his wife Joanne and their two children, Christy and Brian. They have a married daughter, Connie, who teaches school in Oregon.